RAISING FUTURE ADULTS: PLAYING THE LONG GAME

How You Can Help Ensure Your Children Grow Up to be Thriving Adults

David Krasky

This book is dedicated to my children and all other children growing up in this generation

ACKNOWLEDGEMENTS

I'd like to thank all of the mental health professionals, authors and speakers who've focused their work on the improvement of children's lives

ABOUT THE AUTHOR

David Krasky is a licensed school psychologist with over 20 years of working with kids, teens and young adults. He has worked in both public and private school settings with an emphasis on the assessment, treatment and collaboration for a diverse population of children and families.

CONTENTS

PARENTING AND BEHAVIOR

SOCIAL/EMOTIONAL FUNCTIONING

ACADEMIC PERFORMANCE

PARENTING AND BEHAVIOR

Parenting for a Marathon, Not a Sprint

In a fast-paced world, it is hard to remember that life is a marathon, not a sprint. If we go as fast as we can all the time, we will burn out. Moreover, if we are only looking at a few meters in front of us, we'll lose focus on the ultimate goal. In the case of parenting, it is to raise well-adjusted, independent, hard-working, respectful adults. Like in life, parenting is a marathon, not a sprint.

We have (roughly) eighteen years to ensure that our children can survive on their own. While surviving on their own looks different than thirty years ago, it's not that different. Children still have to learn how to wake up on their own, show up on time, solve daily problems, interact with other people, take care of their health and stay safe. If we (parents) keep these big-picture ideas in mind, it makes day-to-day decision making easier.

Here are a few tips when instilling these skills into our children:

1. Think of the end game.

We are always practicing, even as adults. Don't look at your children's failures as an end point, but as a launching point. Their failures are just missed free throws or mistakes on their way to proficiency. Remind yourself and them that they are practicing to develop better habits and that the pressure will be somewhat alleviated when they focus on growth instead of success and failure.

2. Baby Steps.

Goals can be overwhelming when children are far from accomplishing them. Start small. If you want your child to be able to do their homework on their own, start by having them do one or two problems on their own and then increase how much they can complete independently over time. If you want your child to have healthier eating habits, start by cutting or adding one thing for a few weeks, such as soda or fruit.

3. Be a team.

When you go to a hospital, you get a team of doctors. When you have a project at work, there is usually a team working on individual parts. This same approach can be used when teaching our children life-long skills. The team doesn't just have to consist of one or both parents, but the children themselves. If they feel like they are part of the team and not just being told what to do all the time, there is a greater chance of their willingness to work towards life-long habits and goals.

4. Practice what you preach.

I'm as guilty as many others when I say that I often forget to slow down. Practicing and modeling self-care will help keep your own tank full. There should be self-care activities built into every day for you and your children. Whether it is getting your nails done, reading in a quiet area, watching a show or going for a walk, we must give our bodies and brains a break from the stressors of everyday life.

When runners train for a long race, they don't start by running the full 26.2 miles. They start small and learn how to keep a pace that their bodies can endure for the full race. Parenting is similar in that if we don't pace ourselves, we will burn out. We must remind ourselves that the goal is to raise independent, well-adjusted, hard-working young adults who can solve their own problems. It's easier to hand them the iPad when they are upset, but it's more beneficial for them to learn how to self-soothe. It's easier to let them eat whatever they want, but it's more beneficial for them to learn healthy eating habits. By remembering what our goals as parents are, we will be more inclined to make decisions based on our children's future, not just the first few miles of the race.

Raising Grown Ups, Not Just Adults

Most of us were told that becoming an adult came with all of these responsibilities and expectations. Getting a job, paying bills, taking care of our health, etc. What most of us were not taught was how to be a grown-up, not just an adult. In the U.S., once you're 18-years-old, you are considered an adult. Grown-ups, however, are those adults who develop skills to not just think in terms of "right now" but consider how their behavior impacts themselves and others in the future.

There is a new trend of teenagers and young adults who are apprehensive about becoming grown-ups. Some have coined the phrase *failure-to-launch* while others see it as a result of immaturity. Regardless of the cause, the ultimate goal is to raise our children in a way that teaches them how to manage their own lives. This includes problem-solving (not always on their own), self-advocating, asking for help, planning and prioritizing and taking care of their own physical, emotional and social well-being.

Here are some helpful tips for raising fully functioning grown-ups:

1. Real World Consequences.

Most parents' automatic response to any rule-breaking behavior is to take away something...usually their child's phone, iPad or video game. We have to shift our thinking in terms of what we want our children to learn about how their own choices and behaviors impact them. Their bosses won't take away their phones if they don't submit a project or show up to work on time. Here are some examples of how to use real-world consequences:

Woke up late = arrive late to school and have to make up work they missed.

Didn't study for test = poor grade, needs to ask for extra credit, has less free time because they need to do more studying for next test.

Stayed up too late = went to school tired, felt physically bad all day, didn't get to see friends after school because they needed to sleep.

2. Dispel Myths.

Most budding adults share their fear about not being a kid anymore. It's always interesting to dig into what they think happens when you become an adult. Most are nervous about having more responsibilities and expectations and don't realize that perception and reality are often far apart. So be pragmatic. Explain exactly what society expects from them and what it entails. For example, if they think paying bills will be difficult, show them how to use online banking. If they are worried they have to behave differently, ask what they mean and show them examples of how adults can still have fun and be responsible at the same time.

3. Model.

You'll often hear this from professionals who work with children, but it is true that our children are always watching how we communicate and behave. If you are having a difficult time or are under any kind of stress, talk to them about how you're feeling and what you think is the best course of action (age appropriately of course). Model problem-solving, collaboration and communication so they can begin to internalize these habits.

4. Help Them Along.

All children develop differently. This is also true for adults. There are some teenagers who can already live on their own and take care of themselves just like there are some young adults that still need to live at home and require additional support. If the ultimate goal is to have them become independent, well-functioning grown-ups, take small steps when teaching new skills. One of these steps might be finding outside help, so get comfortable in asking for resources and referrals.

The only thing we can all count on in life is getting older, which can be scary and overwhelming but also exciting and unpredictable. While the world around us continues to change, children having to learn how to navigate and thrive within the world has not. Let's help our children on their journey into adulthood and focus on raising grown-ups, not just adults.

Stress to Impress: Tips Based on the Surgeon General's Advisory About High Levels of Parent Stress

According to the Surgeon General's Advisory regarding parent stress, parents are more likely to report high levels of stress when compared to nonparents over the past ten years. In 2023, 33% of parents reported high levels of stress in the past month compared to 20% of adults without children. When stress is severe or prolonged, it can have a deleterious effect; 41% of parents say that most days they are so stressed they cannot function and 48% say that most days their stress is completely overwhelming compared to other adults (20% and 26%, respectively). Now enough of the data. It should come as no surprise that many parents are struggling. Expectedly, if you look at rates of adolescent and teenage anxiety and depression, you'll find very similar numbers. A dear friend of mine always used to say, "If you plant an apple tree, you're not going to get pears."

It should also come as no surprise that with the advancements in technology and social media, higher academic demands and "helicopter" parenting, parental stress continues to grow. Here's the good news! Kids haven't really changed much regarding their needs and development. All children require the same experiences and basic needs to develop the necessary prerequisite skills in order to be fully functioning adults. Kids NEED social experiences. They NEED to be outside to explore. They also NEED to practice being independent and learn how to problem solve by making mistakes and trying out solutions. Sound familiar? That's because we needed the same things when we were growing up.

Now, getting back to parental stress and how severe it has become, there is good news. Experts have been researching these topics for decades and found some great ways you can begin the journey of alleviating some of the overburdening responsibilities of being a parent:

1. Prioritize Parenting.

It's time we value parenting as much as we value earning enough money to be a caregiver. Even though this is a capitalistic-driven society and many people live paycheck to paycheck, the dividends of spending time with your children will pay off...even financially! Think of it this way. If you bookmark specific days/times for quality parent-child interactions, you are reducing the future chance of child maladjustment, stress, social deficits, etc., thereby saving money for intensive interventions and preventing stress in the future.

2. It Takes a Village.

I hate clichés, however, this one is more apt than ever. As a parent of two children, I can tell you firsthand that I am often the one offering rides, promoting get-togethers and coordinating times parents and their children can all get together. When asking why other parents try to do so much on their own, they often share either their own fears or the desire to spend as much time with their children because of their hectic schedules. Fair enough, but to what end and what is the cost?

3. Open Dialogue.

Parents need to be more upfront with how stressful parenting can be. There is no manual on raising children and limited guidance on how we can work together as parents. When thinking about why we are more stressed, one idea is that our generation of parents is more involved in their children's lives (e.g., grades, course selection, activities, monitoring their social media and technology usage, Life360, etc.). Let's talk to each other about the stress that comes along with parenting and how we can find ways and change mindsets, focusing on enjoying being a parent while still being responsible for our children's well-being.

4. So Lonely.

We also need some of the same things our children do. As part of the surgeon general's advisory panel, research found that loneliness and isolation were extremely high for parents and, which often leads to increases in stress levels. While there are plenty of parents who generally enjoy their alone time, the majority of parents need at least some time to connect with others during their stress-filled weeks. Try Inviting a family over for dinner during the week. If you're able, hire a babysitter and go out for a few hours with your spouse, friend(s) or colleagues. Stay a few minutes later at a birthday party to get to know other parents.

While there has been so much focus on the childhood mental health epidemic, we've learned that parents are dealing with some of the highest levels of stress in the past few decades. A more positive way to look at it is that parents wouldn't be stressed if they didn't care so greatly about their children's well-being, which is great...however, if we don't start taking care of ourselves, these numbers will only go up. Lastly, remember that we are always serving as role models for our children on how to not only deal with stress, but to prevent it by practicing healthy, self-caring habits.

The name of this article is a play on a somewhat popular Roblox game called "Dressed to Impress". I thought it was clever, not according to my teenager though.

Surgeon General Advisory on Parent Stress

https://www.hhs.gov/sites/default/files/parents-under-pressure.pdf

Going From Warden To Coach

When it comes to getting our kids to do what we want, the most popular consequences have been the following:

- Confiscation of cell phone

- Taking away video game privileges

- Not letting them access social media

- Not allowing them to see friends

While these probably work in the short term, they aren't as effective in teaching children and teens better ways to deal with being told "no." These terms can be generalized to school, building self-discipline, sleep and eating habits, family relationships, etc. Here are some helpful ideas to stop feeling like a warden and start feeling like a coach:

1. Change your language.

By using terms such as *what works* and *what doesn't*, our children will be less defensive and more open to change. Teens automatically go into shut-down mode when they hear *NO*.

An example can be something like, "So when you stay on your phone right before bed, you have a really hard time waking up. It looks like that is not working, so we're going to try something different," or "Gaming only on weekends has really worked with you getting your school work done more efficiently."

2. Use evidence.

In sessions with children and parents, it is very effective to use objectivity and in most cases, data. It is very difficult for children to argue with the facts when they are very compelling.

"So when you go outside more, you've slept and eaten better and are reportedly in a better mood. It looks like that works and staying inside gaming all day does not." Or "When you get your work done before you log on, you have less incomplete homework... looks like that works better."

17

3. Start small.

When parents try to implement sudden, big changes, there is less of a chance of follow-through and adaptability. It is much like changing one's diet. Most people who try to completely change their diet on Monday are gung-ho for a few days, maybe weeks, but often revert back to their old eating habits. If we make small changes, or tweaks, it doesn't sound as horrible.

So instead of saying, "NO MORE FORTNITE!" you can start with, "After 12:00 PM, there won't be gaming, so you can play from wake up time until noon, but then we need to fill our time with other things."

4. Help teach balance.

Teaching our children what works often leads to a healthy balance between leisure and work.

This can be applied to different aspects of life, such as alone time versus family time, eating healthy versus eating fun food and technology time versus screen-free time. We can teach by modeling and by reinforcing the rules. Here is where the positive outcomes guide their behavior because children will see that the balance is more effective in the long run.

Don't get me wrong, there needs to be rules. We need rules such as no technology before bed or having a balanced diet because children's frontal lobes are not ready to self-monitor and self-regulate yet. But we can implement these rules with consistency and collaboration. Children will know that we have their best interests at heart. Always remember that the goal is for them to create and implement their own rules once they are on their own.

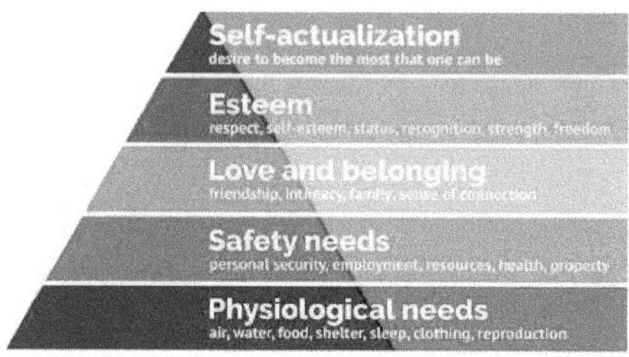

Maslow's hierarchy of needs

Starting From Bottom Up: Parenting in the Right Direction

When thinking about taking care of our children, it can be overwhelming. Between making sure they are healthy, helping them navigate life's stressors and worrying about their safety, etc., we can have a hard time knowing what to "worry about" first. Using a bottom-up approach can help parents determine what is most important, which is why having a hierarchy or way to prioritize needs can be very helpful (see Maslow's hierarchy of needs above). Here are some simple ways to help us decide where to start when developing healthy parenting patterns:

1. Sleep, Eat, Exercise.

When I first meet kids and their families to gather background information, I always ask how they sleep and eat and if they get enough exercise. It is often the case that one or more of these areas are wanting. When picking and choosing battles, these areas should be non-negotiable. If basic health needs aren't met, it is hard for children to tap into their full potential.

2. Safety Patrol.

We can drive ourselves crazy when we think about all of the things that can go wrong in childhood. With the bombardment of news and horrific stories about bad things happening to children, it is no wonder why our generation worries about everything. The question shouldn't be whether we can protect our children from everything. It should be, "Are we teaching our children how to be safe without us?" Do they know how to tell whether a person is safe or dangerous? Can they cross a street on their own? Do they know who their "safe" people are in case of emergency?

3. You Are Always Loved.

A question I began asking years ago when it comes to children's feelings of love and acceptance is "When your parents are mad at you, do you think they still love you in that moment?" Many children often answer no. It is hard for some children to understand that a parent can be angry with them and love them at the same time. It is helpful to not only tell our children we love them, but to show them as well, even when we are frustrated and nervous. By using effective communication and objectivity, it can help children understand that consequences have nothing to do with our feelings about them.

4. Self-Esteem is not a 4-Letter Word.

Children born in the 70s and 80s were part of the self-esteem generation. Our happiness and feelings were often the driving force in parental decision-making. What was forgotten was that self-esteem is developed by overcoming obstacles, developing healthy coping and social skills and learning how to problem solve...not by getting a trophy for just showing up. Letting children lose sometimes or feel negative emotions allows them to develop the necessary skills to become more successful over time. Carol Dweck, author of *Mindset*, teaches us that helping children develop a growth mindset allows them to understand that failing is part of learning. Every time we fail, even if we are trying hard, our brains grow, and we get closer and closer to our ultimate goals.

Parenting can be one of the scariest things in the world, especially if we don't know where to start. Maslow's hierarchy of needs can help structure and organize a much larger goal...raising well-adjusted children with perseverance, healthy social and emotional skills and the ability to live a safe and healthy life.

Natural Consequences: Life's Best Teacher

Humans for centuries have learned through natural consequences. Be it burning oneself on a fire or mastering a task after many hours of practice, consequences that are directly related to our own behaviors are often the most reliable and consistent reinforcer. It is only in the last few decades that consequences have become focused on restricting privileges or removing objects that have nothing to do with unwanted behaviors. More often than not, parents will ask for their child's phone or tell their child that they lost their video game or screen time, even if the negative behavior has nothing to do with these activities. These consequences will often work in the short-term but have a limited impact on lasting behavior change.

When choosing consequences for our children's actions, we should always keep in mind what will teach them and ultimately help them improve their behavior in the long run. So here are some useful techniques when implementing natural consequences:

1. Keep your eye on the prize.

For any parent, the ultimate goal is to raise an independent child who makes good and thoughtful decisions. By allowing them to deal with the natural consequences of their choices, they feel the direct effects of those choices, thus leading to more impactful experiences.

Think back to a time when after getting a bad grade, you were not allowed to see your friends until your grade improved. The same idea can be applied to gaming, Netflixing or social media usage.

2. Make the connection.

In the beginning, children will need their parents to connect their actions to the natural consequences. For example, if you leave your toys out, the dog may eat them. If you don't finish your healthy food, you can't have dessert. When you speak to me with that tone of voice, I am unable to listen and respond calmly.

Making these connections early can also help children develop a more balanced and productive life.

3. Be respectful.

That goes for us! Not them. This means that the consequence shouldn't involve shame or humiliation. "Your child already feels bad when he does something wrong," says Dr. Nelsen, author of the *Positive Discipline Series*. "If you say, 'I told you so,' or if you shame him afterward, you'll lessen the potential for learning because he'll stop processing the experience and instead focus on the blame."

4. Give a little to get a little.

It's funny how many children don't understand the idea of increasing their chances of getting what they want. You can remind children, when they start asking for things like going out for ice cream or a new Lego set, that if they follow your rules, their chances of getting what they want improve. When they begin misbehaving or making bad choices, remind them that their natural consequence of, let's say, fighting with their brother all day, would be to not go out in public because they've shown that they can't even get along in private.

Natural consequences don't have to be a thing of the past. We can begin teaching our children at a young age about how their actions affect their future. Remember, we aren't going to be around forever to tell them not to wait until the night before the test to study. One important side note is to remember your child's age and developmental stage. Things like health and safety are going to be your "line in the sand, non-negotiable" areas. If a child is not old enough to walk across a street safely, they must hold the hand of an adult. We can also apply this methodology to older children who need to improve their diet, exercise and sleep patterns.

Thinking Differently About Behavior (Problems)

Ahhhhh… problematic behavior. Parents' final frontier. The one thing that can turn any seemingly innocuous event into an ordeal. There are decades of research and even more interventions and treatments to address unwanted behaviors. Unfortunately, many of the effective treatments cost a lot of money (and time) and require high rates of consistency and follow-through. Before we dig into problematic behavior, let's define it because it's not so black and white. First of all, a behavior might be fine in one environment and completely unacceptable in a different setting (think calling out in a classroom versus at a sporting event). Behavioral expectations also change as children mature and learn to adapt to the world around them.

Most families and teachers use the same method in dealing with unwanted behaviors. Punishment. That is inflicting a negative consequence that the child (hopefully) finds unpleasurable, thus leading to a decrease in said behavior. Examples can be spanking or taking away a privilege (i.e., phone, video game, etc.). Reinforcement, on the other hand, means you're trying to increase a behavior. For example, every time your child asks for something nicely, you praise them and give them what they asked for. Behaviorists believe that a child's problematic behaviors occur for only a few simple reasons. The most common reasons include getting something they want, like a video game, or avoiding something they don't want, like doing their homework. We've learned that children are much more complicated than that and are affected by other factors such as sleep, diet and activity, along with environmental factors like being exposed to stressful events or information their brains are not ready to interpret.

When it comes to understanding problem behaviors, we must first shift the way we think of them:

1. It's not about you.

When a child is misbehaving, their parents often say things like, "You're making me so upset" or "Why would you do this to me?" The odds are that your child is not thinking about your feelings at that moment, and they shouldn't. You are in charge of your feelings, and they are in charge of theirs.

2. Be an enforcer and teacher, not a warden or dictator.

Children need structure, consistency and routines. Our job is to set limits and boundaries from an early age and enforce them by keeping them accountable with the sole purpose of teaching, not punishing. Punishment, for punishment's sake, isn't teaching and in fact, will often lead to more problematic behavior and relationships in the future. Accountability only means that they are facing whatever predetermined consequences occur once they make their choices. An example might be by choosing not to turn off their device when told they then cannot have the device the next day.

3. Remove yourself.

This has been one of the most effective first steps in any behavioral intervention between children and adults. The chances that two people solve a problem when both parties are upset or in a state of emotional dysregulation are highly unlikely. If your child won't take some space, feel free to go to your own room, go for a drive or a walk around the neighborhood. Try to do this early on within the interaction because once it escalates, this might be more difficult to do safely.

4. Use unemotional language.

Most children will tell you after they misbehave that they know what they did was wrong or unacceptable. They don't need more reminders of how "bad" they are. Instead, use phrases like "this is or is not working, let's find a different way or we'll keep working on it." This will help the child not feel rejected and that you are both working as a team.

Punishment is baked into our culture. Most parents' first go-to when children aren't compliant is to "take away" something. What is not baked in is our desire to prevent problematic behaviors by discovering the root cause for the behavior in the first place and using more objective and direct language. This is much easier said than done. Dealing with problematic behaviors is one of the greatest stressors in parenting and requires practice, patience and oftentimes, collaboration. If you feel that you need to improve these skills, find a professional who specializes in parent-child interactions.

Hope for the Best, Plan for the Worst: Preventing and Coping with Extreme Behaviors

According to the Child Mind Institute, "It's useful to think of a tantrum as a reaction to a situation a child can't handle in a more grown-up way—say, by talking about how he feels, or making a case for what he wants, or just doing what he's been asked to do. Instead, he is overwhelmed by emotion. And if unleashing his feelings in a dramatic way — crying, yelling, kicking the floor, punching the wall, or hitting a parent — serves to get him what he wants (or out of whatever he was trying to avoid), it's a behavior that he may come to rely on " (https://childmind.org/article/how-to-handle-tantrums-and-meltdowns/).

For many children with a diagnosis of ADHD, a

dysregulation disorder, or any other disorder that impacts the emotional control areas of their brains, once they've arrived at the point of no return, there is little that can be done with regard to using punishment or reinforcement that is consistently effective. In this article, we will discuss ways to generate preventative solutions along with what caregivers can do once the child is in a state of complete emotional/behavioral dysregulation:

1. Know the triggers and have a plan.

With most children, the causes for these "meltdowns" are pretty obvious, such as having to turn off their device, being told no, or having to do something they don't like (i.e., homework or doing something boring/anxiety-provoking). If it is not one of these more common causes, do a little detective work with your child (when they are in a calm and rational state) by asking them after they've calmed down what was causing them to be so upset. Once you establish specific triggers, you can start to put plans in place for when it happens again... because it most likely will.

2. Preparation.

It's helpful to prepare children before the triggering event by giving them a heads-up while also asking what they plan to do if they become upset. It may sound something like, "When you stop playing Fortnite after your next loss, what's your plan if you get very upset? Remember, if you start negotiating or refuse to turn off the game, you're then choosing to not play tomorrow. If you turn off the game when I ask, you get to play tomorrow." Help them brainstorm some ways to transition off of the game. Examples include doing something else they find fun or interesting or engaging in a family activity.

3. Take space.

Most parents have a very difficult time remaining calm and collected when their child is in the middle of a meltdown. It's human nature to become emotionally activated if those around us are getting louder, angrier and/or even aggressive. So the best thing to do is... leave. The odds are your child won't remove themselves so they can calm down on their own so you'll have to instead. Be prepared for them to follow you so have a plan of either getting out of the house (if they are old enough) or finding an area in the house in which you can calm yourself down. If they begin banging on your door, ignore them until they calm down and stop. Think of it like riding out a storm (put on your headphones and hope that nothing breaks).

4. Learning and Growing.

Once your child has calmed down to the point where you can speak with them rationally, ask them (calmly) what is going on that led to such extreme behavior. If they don't know, you can point out some things you noticed and tell them that the two of you will continue to work on dealing with being upset. Use "growth mindset" terms such as "continuing to work on" or "getting better at" when talking about their behavioral reactions. Always finish the conversation by reminding them that you will always love them and that everyone gets very upset sometimes.

Dealing with severe behaviors is one of the most difficult challenges for parents. Oftentimes, we feel unprepared and reactionary, which almost always leads to escalation. By preparing and having plans in place, you won't be able to prevent every extreme behavioral reaction, but over time, you'll reduce behaviors in both frequency and severity. Your children will also be learning life-long skills for their own behavioral and emotional growth.

One Size Does Not Fit All

It would be great if every intervention worked perfectly… for every person…all the time! A world where working out always prevented heart attacks, washing hands always prevented the flu and studying always resulted in As. Unfortunately, nothing is ever 100% guaranteed. However, we CAN increase our chances of success. Helping children find what works best for their emotional, social and educational needs can lead to well-adjusted, independent children.

To do so, we need to start shifting our mindset and language. Our mindset must be one of teacher and researcher (or data collector), while our language must reflect a nonjudgmental, encouraging collaboration. This may be a challenging transition because our culture tends to focus on what "doesn't" work or what children are doing wrong. Here are some simple tips to help your children find what works:

1. Use simple language.

Using terms such as "that doesn't look like it's working too well" or "what do you think might work better" taps into their problem-solving brains instead of the problem-blaming process. Look into growth mindset terms to get some more ideas on how to promote trying something new or different rather than giving up (see below).

2. Use data.

Data doesn't only have to be quantitative. It's usually easier to use your eyes and ears to pick up on any changes in your child's behaviors. Helping children learn that they often exhibit patterns of emotional responses can help them begin to develop new coping skills. The same can be applied to academic or social achievement. Showing your children how and when they are most effective can be measured by grades, but also by their overall mood, willingness to engage with others, voice tone and the way in which they cope with stressors.

3. Tech by Doing.

One of the easiest ways to help children implement a problem-solving method to promote success is to start doing it yourself. If you're getting frustrated with your child because they are not listening or giving you an attitude, you can say, "This isn't working. You sound frustrated and I'm starting to feel angry, so we need to take a break."

4. Fill that toolbox.

By finding what works, children are beginning to create a toolbox of coping skills and solution-based strategies that work best for them. After enough practice and feedback, children should be able to tell you what works best for studying, learning, self-calming, problem solving and communication. Examples may be studying with a friend instead of on their own, discussing difficult topics over the weekend instead of during the week when they are more stressed because of school demands, or dealing with stress by engaging in an active instead of passive activity like playing, exercising, reading or doing something creative.

Research has shown that focusing on the positive rather than negative has longer-lasting and more positive outcomes. Now don't misconstrue that into thinking children don't need discipline... they do (i.e., consistent rules, boundaries, limits and consequences). However, helping children find what works best to produce their greatest chances of success will foster

more independence and confidence in their own
abilities to deal with any challenge that comes their
way.

Getting Comfortable with Discomfort: How Growth is Usually Painful, but Necessary

In the gym, there are clichéd phrases like "big gains" or "no pain, no gain." As cringe-worthy as they may sound when you are working out, they are the simplification of an important theory.

Change or growth is often painful. In this context, however, we will use the term 'uncomfortable' instead of painful. Many children seen in my office have spent years avoiding discomfort, thus resulting in continued stagnation of skills (coping, social, physical, academic, etc.). Their mindset is often fixed in the belief that they are the way they are and they cannot change that.

The theory of growth mindset teaches us that our underlying beliefs about our intelligence and learning affect our effort and output. Recent neuroscientific discoveries have shown us that children can increase their neural growth by actions such as employing useful strategies, asking questions, practicing new habits and adopting a healthy diet and sleep pattern.

Let's take this further and apply it to the emotional and behavioral functioning of children. Anxious children avoid situations that evoke a fear response. Unfortunately, most will not just outgrow this pattern of behavior and will continue to avoid situations that they perceive as anxiety-provoking. In other words, the only way to get over your fear of flying is to eventually get on an airplane. Certainly, you can work up to that goal by gradual exposure, learning better coping skills and reframing thoughts, but no matter what... you'll have to, at some point, get on that plane.

That being said, here are some quick ideas on promoting growth by embracing a little discomfort:

1. Discomfort eventually gets more comfortable.

With most things that are uncomfortable, the more you do it, the more comfortable it becomes.

Public speaking, working out or even going to a party can initially be very anxiety-provoking.

Remind your children that they will be uncomfortable at first, but it will get better at dealing with these events over time. Encourage their effort to sit with their discomfort rather than giving up. With time and patience, the discomfort will dissipate and transform into growth.

2. Be honest.

My daughter hates shots. Ever since that first one—and believe me, she remembers—her automatic thought when about to receive a shot is heightened anxiety. Even as a teenager, she still asks if it will hurt. Most parents say things like, "No! It's just a little pinch" or "It doesn't hurt me." A better technique is to be honest and reinforce the idea that while it is going to hurt, pain (discomfort) is temporary. This is true for any situation that is uncomfortable. You can tell them that it might hurt but only for a little bit. You can even apply this to school work. Studying or working hard is often uncomfortable at first until the child builds their mental stamina. Help them learn that it may be uncomfortable for a little, but they will eventually get used to working hard. You can even remind them that their brain is growing (neuroplasticity).

3. Discomfort is often good.

Even though I'm not a fan of the terms "good" and "bad", they are easy for children to understand. Without discomfort, they might not try something new that they eventually love or feel the pride that comes with overcoming obstacles. Another good thing about discomfort is that it helps build resilience and grit, key characteristics in children who eventually become successful adults.

4. Learning when to ask for help.

Oftentimes teenagers come to the realization that they've always had someone doing things for them or preventing any discomfort (think helicopter parents). My question to them is: what happens when they go off on their own?

Discomfort will help teach children how to self-advocate by learning what works best for them. Some children will come to the realization that they need a tutor for math, a trainer for the gym, a friend to study with or a counselor to talk to. Without being a little uncomfortable, they will never be given the opportunity to reach out for help.

It is natural for parents to want to minimize discomfort in their children. There is an evolutionary instinct that heightens our stress levels when our children are stressed. By reframing our thoughts of discomfort as opportunities for growth, we can help our children become more resilient and self-reliant, likely leading to healthier rates of self-esteem and worth.

"Discomfort encourages change, which propels us to grow. So, by that theory, discomfort is necessary."

You Can't Be Happy All The Time: Why It's Important to Let Children Experience All Emotions

"But I just want him to be happy" is a phrase often said by parents of toddlers, children, teens, and even adults. Unfortunately, this is an unrealistic and perhaps counterproductive goal. Happiness is a feeling, and feelings don't last forever. Therefore, children can't always be happy. In fact, it's more beneficial for children's emotional growth if they experience a wide range of normal emotions. These include anger, sadness, frustration, guilt, fear, and loss. The only way children can learn how to cope with these feelings is through exposure and practice. How can kids learn how to deal with being upset if they're never given the opportunity to feel upset?

Instead of wanting our children to always be happy, let's shift our focus to having them learn how to deal with all emotions in an age-appropriate, healthy manner. This will eventually lead to an overall sense of peace, maturity, and self-reliance. Here are some simple tips for caregivers to help promote healthy coping skills in their children:

1. Let them feel their feelings.

Instead of trying to assuage their uncomfortable feelings by bribing, negotiating or downplaying, let them be upset. As long as they are not hurting themselves or anyone else, this will be an important step in their emotional growth. Children as young as two years old can begin learning how to self-regulate when upset.

2. Remind them (and yourself) that this is temporary.

Nobody likes the sound of their child crying or whining, or the sound of any child crying or whining for that matter. We have to remind our children that whatever negative emotion they are feeling will eventually go away. It is also important to remind ourselves of that as well. Set a timer, walk away, lock yourself in your room if you have to so you don't get tempted to relieve their discomfort without giving them a chance to self-calm as well as serving as a positive role model.

3. Teach them what to do.

Feeling upset is a great opportunity for children to learn how to better cope with feeling upset. There are an infinite amount of strategies children can practice and put into their "coping toolbox," such as taking time to be alone, reading, going outside, taking a bath, calling a friend, etc. Just make sure that before your child decides to watch YouTube for six hours as their coping skill, they understand that the goal of a coping skill is to reduce their negative emotional response, not to stare at a screen for the rest of the day. Also, ensure that they have enough coping skills that are unique to specific situations like car rides, new experiences, school, community activities, etc.

4. Strive for peace, not happiness.

While happiness is temporary, feeling at peace can be long-lasting. Peace can be achieved in several ways, but one easy way is to have children focus on things they have, not things they want; and that emotions are temporary and can be navigated by acceptance and practice. Understanding that we can change our mindsets through practice and consistency. And that as we mature, we will soon develop a greater sense of purpose and self-awareness that will lead to better emotional resilience.

When you really think about it, we don't want our kids to always be happy...we want them to be at peace. We want them to have the emotional capability to deal with any feelings they experience. We want them to have healthy coping skills and self-worth. We want them to be able to advocate for themselves and do what is right. We want them to work hard but understand that we all have strengths and weaknesses. And we want them to understand that it's not our job to make them happy; it's our job to make sure they know how to deal with NOT being happy.

You Are the Reward: Using Positive Attention to Shape Behaviors and Improve the Parent-Child Relationship

The only job I can think of that is similar to a parent is a bomb defuser. Both have to be calm, talk evenly and at any moment and be ready for everything to blow up at any minute. And that's what it feels like sometimes, a job rather than a privilege. That's partly because parents aren't explicitly taught anything about behavior or development and are simultaneously dealing with more external factors that make parenting more complicated and stressful.

In behaviorism, it is taught that there are antecedents, behaviors and consequences. That's it! A child doesn't follow directions, they are put in time-out. A student studies for their test, they get a good grade. One of the most important reinforcers, however, remains positive parent attention. Positive parental attention that is genuine and targeted is one of the best ways to shape behaviors, not only because it's free, but because most children of all ages still want their parents' approval. As children get older it can also be used as a way to teach self-calming and emotional regulation. At the same time, you are using fewer threats and punishment. Here are some easy ways to use attention as a reward or model to improve child behavior:

1. Walk away.

Rather than get into a battle or negotiation with your child, tell them you'll come back when they are ready to listen or follow directions. The same strategy can be used if they begin acting or speaking in a manner you find unacceptable. Make sure language is simple and direct ("I'll come back when you're ready to follow directions" or "You sound upset, come get me when you've cooled down"). This also goes for the parent. It's reasonable to say something like, "I'm getting very frustrated and don't want to yell, so I need some time to myself."

2. You're a better reward than

(*insert any screen time activity or tangible item*).

As much as children love Minecraft, Roblox, TikTok and YouTube, joint activities and attention with their parent(s) are irreplaceable. More so for children under the age of twelve. Doing something with them can be just as if not more rewarding them doing it without you. Better yet, try doing something with them that they enjoy, like playing their favorite video game together or making your own silly video.

3. Attention means attention.

This means no texting or scrolling through the phone while giving your child your undivided attention. Just being there is good, but not as good as being actively engaged and present. Ask open-ended questions about what they are doing or how they achieved something. If you are praising positive behaviors, be specific. Also, don't make it about how you feel. For example, "It makes me happy when you_____." or "When you don't follow directions, it makes me sad."). This should be about them.

4. You can use it anywhere.

That's the great thing about attention! It can be a simple smile, hug, a funny quip or even a head nod acknowledging their good choices. These examples can be used anywhere with any age group and are all ways to increase their positive behavior along with the child/parent bond.

Research has shown over and over again that positive reinforcement has more beneficial long-term outcomes than negative reinforcement or punishment. That is not to say children should not be accountable for their actions, but the consequence should be the change agent, not your attention or love. Ignoring should not be used as a source of punishment, but if you feel like you might do or say something harmful to your child, share with them that you need some time to cool down. This is not ignoring, it is modeling self-calming. It also lets them know that you don't want to yell and punish and that it's hard for any human, child or parent, to regulate their behaviors when upset. Parenting is hard, stressful and tiring. It is also amazing, rewarding and life-changing. We should remember to use time-tested strategies that are easy and effective. Because more than anything else, our children want our love, approval... and attention.

Is It OK to Compromise with Your Kids?

"Five more minutes!" The ever-echoing plea from the hopeful child whose goal is to squeeze as much gaming, watching or playing as possible from their parents. Compromising with children isn't new. Previous generations wanted more time outside before dinner or to be able to drive a little farther away than our parents were comfortable. While compromising with children isn't new, there are new factors that parents face. An evolving technological revolution, increased academic demands and helicopter parenting make parenting more complicated than ever; however, one thing still remains. Children and parents will disagree on what children want and what parents believe they need.

If we think of raising children as really just raising future adults, compromising can be an asset rather than a parenting cop-out. Compromising teaches compromising. It also promotes a more flexible style that can lead to a more peaceful household. Now, some things should not be compromised (e.g., health-related or safety issues). If you have a rule about your children getting a specific number of hours of sleep on school nights, be steadfast. Obviously there will be extenuating circumstances, but for the most part, you'll want to be firm with this one because decreased sleep is strongly associated with mood, attentional and behavioral problems. We even have to think of their "screen health" as well and set firm limits with technology.

Here are some examples of when compromising can be very useful and get your children to "mostly" follow directions:

1. Forced Choices.

This is one of the most effective ways to get children, teens (and even adults) to do what you've asked of them. Forced choices provide two or even three options in which the child must choose one. Examples include which vegetables they want to eat with dinner, where they want to complete homework or what book they want to read to complete their required reading time.

This is also very effective for turning off electronics. It would look something like, "You can choose to turn off the game now and play more tomorrow or keep playing, I turn it off, and you don't get to play tomorrow."

2. Balancing Act.

Like much of parenting, there are lots of gray areas in which parents must balance between punitive and permissive parenting. Parents frequently want to feel a sense of control and respect and often react emotionally when feeling them slip away. An easy way to recalibrate during an impasse should include natural consequences and options for the child so that they learn from their positive and negative choices.

3. No Choice.

Even when there appear to be no choices, there are still some. A child can refuse to eat or get in the car. Some might even run away from you with their phone or tablet after being told to hand it over, leading to extreme reactions and consequences. These are the times in which you have to remind yourself, and your children, that they are "choosing" to not follow directions and any consequences will be due to their choice. If they don't get in the car to go to school, then they don't get to do anything of privilege at home (gaming, phone, eating good food, sleeping, etc.). Run away with the phone? Use your provider's service to disable the phone. Remind them that once they comply, you can start talking about how they can earn the things they want.

4. Think Before You Act.

This actually goes for the parent, not the child. We have a tendency to say "no" before getting all of the information. I'm guilty of this as children aren't the best communicators and once you start getting more information, it's a little easier to compromise to a satisfactory solution. This is useful for occasions when your child wants to meet up with new friends or do something without adult supervision for the first time. There is a difference between going to a carnival and going to a carnival...with their friends.....at an elementary school....with lots of supervision....and safe rides. See! If they shared all the facts first, you'd probably be more apt to say yes.

So getting back to the initial question, is it ok to compromise with your children? Yes, with a caveat. Compromising over things that don't have as many long-term negative consequences can teach flexibility and independence; however, there also needs to be some strong lines in the sand regarding health, safety and building strong habits for the future. We also must remember that learning to compromise will only improve their social skills and independence, leading to healthier and more productive lives.

TMI

Many parents, myself included, have to deal with our own mental health issues. While going through my own ups and downs, I frequently wonder, "How much should I share about what I'm going through with my children?" There are millions of parents in our country who struggle daily with their own mental health issues. Previous generations either rarely spoke about topics such as anxiety, depression or burnout, or minimized their symptoms. Fortunately, the pendulum seems to be swinging in the right direction, with the new generations taking a greater interest in their own and others' emotional well-being.

Like most topics, when deciding what to share about yourself with your child will depend on several factors, including age, maturity, development and their own emotional well-being. Here are some quick tips to help guide you when you're unsure what to share and how to share it:

1. Know your child.

Some children, depending more on maturity and development, will be able to handle learning that their parent is or has dealt with their own mental illness or instability. If your child is extremely sensitive and internalizes everything, don't go into too much detail and always focus on what you are doing to get better.

2. Age and maturity.

For younger children, keep it simple with statements such as "Daddy isn't feeling too great and needs to rest tonight." As children get older, they might be more perceptive and know something is wrong, so be honest, but don't overwhelm them. You can let them know that you're dealing with (insert characteristic here, such as more anxiety or sadness than usual) but always reiterate that you are getting help and it is not their fault.

3. Be ready for questions.

Younger children might want to know how you "got it" or how it can be fixed, while older children may ask if the same thing will happen to them one day. If you're unsure how to answer these questions, reach out to your therapist or go to some reputable websites such as the National Institute of Mental Health or the National Alliance on Mental Illness.

4. Reassurance.

More than anything, children need to know that you'll be ok. This all boils down to this main idea. Take this opportunity to show them how to get help, take care of their own emotional well-being and treat this as if they were to treat a medically related issue (i.e., building a strong team and using data and research).

We all have our own "stuff." Sometimes, it intensifies and requires additional treatment and support. Our children will most likely be aware that something is going on, so be prepared to share it in a developmentally appropriate manner with emphasis on your plan to get better. If you or your spouse is dealing with something more intense that requires a higher level of care, consider having your child speak with a mental health professional.

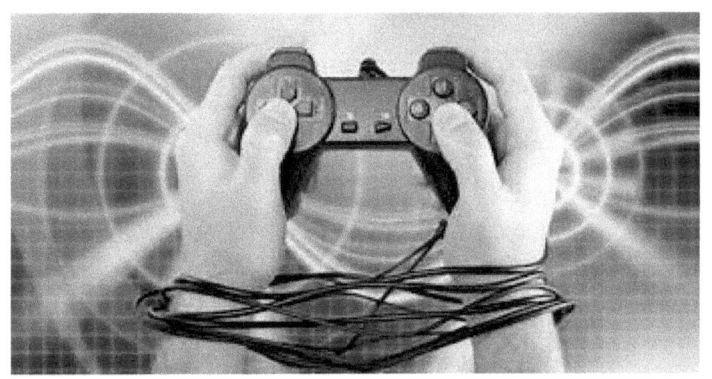

How Much Is Too Much Video Gaming?

While this isn't the first generation to grow up with technological entertainment, it is definitely one of the first to cause significant deficits in their social and behavioral well-being. The word *addiction* has been used often when parents describe their children's dependence on gaming. According to the American Psychological Association, gaming addiction is when at least five of the following nine characteristics are observed for at least one year: gaming preoccupation, withdrawal, tolerance, loss of interest in other activities, downplaying use, loss of relationship, educational or career opportunities, gaming to escape or relieve anxiety, guilt, or other negative mood states, failure to control or continued gaming despite psychosocial problems.

One of the biggest problems of video games isn't the games themselves, but the time they take away from necessary social and environmental experiences. Another challenge parents face is the evolution of gaming, which focuses on keeping users on the game as long as possible by using methods such as frequent updates, multiplayer modes with voice interaction, competitions, and so on. On the other hand, a healthy amount of gaming can be beneficial for kids. Especially those who use gaming as a way to connect with others and have a fun stress-relieving activity built into their day. Like noted earlier, if you start seeing signs of gaming becoming a problem, you want to discuss with your child your role as their parent in helping rebalance their gaming and non-gaming activities. Here are some tips when thinking about your children and gaming:

1. Set Limits And Stick To Them.

This should always be the first step. No matter what age your children begin gaming, set limits and stick to them. If they are unable to comply with the limits, then the child is not mature enough to engage with the game. A good rule of thumb is to have a balanced ratio of gaming and non-gaming time (i.e., two hours of outdoor play = two hours of game time) with a limit for both school and non-school days.

2. Natural Consequences.

If a child is unable to turn off the game when they are told or secretly game when no one is around, a natural consequence is they cannot be on video games the following day.

Again, follow step one. Set the limit, stick to it and enforce it.

3. Replace

It is always easier to replace a behavior than to stop it. Make sure your children have lots of different hobbies, activities, etc., so that when gaming time is up, they have something else they can do and enjoy. Older children can get a part-time job, even if it is within the neighborhood, such as dog walking/sitting, babysitting, etc. For younger children, be available if your child needs you to go outside with them.

4. Be Involved.

Even though most adults are not gamers or can even keep up with the complexity of most games (me included), we can at least learn the nuances of the games our children play. Are they MMORPG (massive multiplayer online role-playing games) or FPS (first-person shooters)? Are your children communicating with friends, strangers, etc.? Do they play competitively or just as a hobby?

Gaming will not go away any time soon, so we as parents have to ensure that our children learn how to set their own limits to prevent any long-term problems. While gaming has its positive attributes, too much of anything can eventually become a problem (even too much working out is not good for you). So whether you are a parent or a professional working with parents, remember that it is our job as adults to create healthy limits and boundaries.

Practice Makes Perfect Better

Practice does not make perfect, but it can definitely make any skill better. Coaches demand constant repetition until their players execute without error. The same goes for teachers, tutors, directors, musicians or any other professional whose role is to shape their students' habits. The hardest part of change usually occurs in the beginning. Brains like to keep the status quo.

Once those neural connections are made, it takes a bit of effort to break them and create new ones. However, neuroplasticity research has taught us that brains can improve and change with effort, consistency and time. In this article, we will review how you can help your children develop new habits or change any unwanted habits:

1. Start small:

Dramatic changes can be overwhelming and even paralyzing to children and adults. By starting with small changes, the first step doesn't seem too difficult for their brains to adapt to. For example:

Diet - cut out one unhealthy item (i.e., soda)

Exercise - walk the dog for 5 minutes

Homework - do the first 3 problems

Screen time - screen-free time while eating

2. Think like a coach:

Athletes are always improving by challenging themselves. For example, while training for a marathon, a runner will increase how many miles they run each week. You can take the same approach with children. If you want your child to be able to do all of their homework without World War III erupting, start small and increase the amount over time.

3. Include the child whenever possible.

Buy-in from the child is as important as consistency from the adult. Decide with your child, when appropriate, what changes they can begin to make.

Give them a few choices so they feel like they have some decision-making and control.

4. It's easier to replace than terminate

Take, for example, a child who feels stressed or bored during homework. They might want to check their social media to alleviate those uncomfortable feelings, but then end up wasting valuable time on the phone. Help them find more effective stress-relieving activities that are also adaptive and helpful. Some examples are:

• Switching tasks

• Changing their location

• Working with a friend

• Going for a walk

Good habits formed in childhood often last through adulthood. However, the same goes for bad habits. Our role as parents has changed since the advent of technology, increased academic demands, 24-hour news cycles, and blurred lines in traditional hierarchies. By taking incremental steps and being consistent, children can learn new habits that will lead to better outcomes. To quote Benny Urquidez, "What you practice, is what you'll do."

Working Hard is Hard Work: Helping Children Learn How to Self-Motivate and Persist Under Pressure

The unfortunate moniker "entitled" has been assigned to many Gen Alpha's and millennials. It used to be called "spoiled," but the meaning behind it remains the same. More and more children live with privileges previous generations did not have. It used to be hard to look up words or find where you're going by reading a map. Google did not solve our math problems. It appears that the new definition of hard work primarily focuses on the amount of homework and tests students have, whereas previous generations found hard work synonymous with what they did outside of school. There are fewer children who have part-time jobs, mow the lawn, take care of their younger siblings and do household chores, all while going to school and keeping their grades up.

Let's be honest, hard work is hard... but that's the point, it's supposed to be. Studying something boring is hard. Putting off gaming until homework is done to the best of your ability is hard. But here's something most children and teens don't know yet. You can get better at working hard.

So much better that it becomes natural, like learning to shoot a basketball or lift a weight, with practice and persistence, they can become as routine as writing your name. We also have placed too much focus on grades or results and not how they got there. Give me a student who gets B's by working his tail off over a student who gets A's while sleeping in class any day. That first student will eventually be able to accomplish anything they put their mind to, while the straight A student will likely get a rude awakening once something gets too "hard."

Most professionals encourage teachers and parents to praise effort and hard work, not results, so here are some helpful ideas to get kids to work harder:

1. Praise Effort, Not the Result.

While many things are not in a child's control, hard work is the one factor that they have complete autonomy over. Now, while measuring hard work is difficult, it is not impossible.

When you see your children working hard (you will know when you see it), make sure you genuinely tell them how proud you are and no matter what grade they receive, they should be proud of themselves. If you're unsure how to measure their output, compare it to something you can measure like a workout or time practicing an instrument.

2. Be Concrete.

You might know what working hard looks like, but your children may not. Some ways to

teach children how to know if they are working hard or not often should focus on doing something different from last time to study or complete an assignment, working on one specific task with fewer distractions (no Snapchat, TikTok, Netflix or Youtube) and assigning a number to how hard they are working. For example, if you ask how hard they studied for their last test, with a 10 being the hardest they've ever worked on something and a 1 being no effort, children can usually answer honestly and accurately.

3. Use Meaningful Examples.

Kids often work hard on the things they enjoy the most. I've personally watched children use maximum effort to beat a video game, build a Lego set or lift a weight. Point out to your children when you see them working hard and let them know that they have the ability to work hard in other areas. It will just take practice. That being said, make sure your children get opportunities to...

4. Practice, practice, practice.

If you practice working hard, you will get better at working hard. With children who need more practice at working hard, use shorter periods. Ask them to give you maximum effort for 5 minutes. Like a muscle, incremental growth will happen over time. By structuring the time they are giving a maximum amount of effort, you will see more buy-in and will have more opportunities to praise their effort. Moreover, they will see their own improvement, thus increasing their willingness to work hard. You're ultimately trying to create a healthy cycle of perpetual success and growth that feed into each other.

Instead of complaining about millennials being entitled or not knowing how to work hard, let's teach them. This generation has been given more opportunities to not have to work hard than any generation before them. How can we fault children who can get information on their phone in less than five seconds, have videos showing them how to solve any problem or are measured by grades and SAT scores instead of life skills and common sense? It sounds like teaching them instead of criticizing them is going to be... hard work!

But I Turned Out Just Fine: Differences Between Generations and Why Parenting Must Evolve

Like most fields of science, parenting has evolved with the acquisition of new data. We've learned that smoking (cigarettes) is bad, exercise is good and the earth is not flat. As knowledgeable as we think we are, we still have a lot of work to do. The world appears to be evolving faster than us. For example, every time we figure out new technology, something better comes out and right when we think we know how to keep our children safe, more threats come to light. However, we keep using the old adage, "My parents did that to me when I was a kid and I turned it fine." If we want to evolve and do better, we must evolve, which means relying on evidence, data and facts.

Here are some things research has confirmed since our childhood to be useful when raising our children:

1. Discipline is good, spanking is not.

Discipline should be synonymous with consistency, and should not come across as being mean or tough. Consistency has been shown time and time again to help improve almost any unwanted behaviors and increase desired ones. When being consistent, the most important factors are using a reinforcer that works, keeping calm and giving children plenty of opportunities to improve. Spanking has been found to not only not work, but to increase the chances that your child will learn to use aggression to affect others' behaviors.

2. Saying "no" is also good.

Many adults complain of the "snowflake" or "entitled" generation, but ask yourself this, who raised them? One of the best ways to raise appreciative, hard-working children is to make them work, wait and earn. For many children, their parents don't like to see them uncomfortable so they jump in to rescue them at the first hint of struggle or discomfort. Make them wait to get the iPad after dinner. Make them save their own money to buy Robux and make them earn new AirPods by working for an allowance.

3. With all these screens, limits are necessary.

A parent once asked me if they should let their child play as much Minecraft as they wanted after school. The child was five. So yeah... that's a hard no. More and more children are missing the opportunities to build necessary life skills through play, socialization and using their imagination. We are quickly realizing that it is almost impossible for most children to self-monitor when it comes to technology due to the immediacy and depth of it. Now more than ever, we must implement strict limits and boundaries.

4. Our goals don't have to be their goals.

Thirty years ago, most of us didn't know there was an option of NOT going to college. Children will be successful if they do what they love... or at least, don't hate. The money will come if they are passionate about what they do and show the work ethic and professionalism most companies and clients seek out. By allowing children to pursue their own goals, you help ensure they don't live a life of hating their jobs or feeling stuck, which can lead to depression, marital discord or resentment. Instead of pushing our agendas, let's collaborate with our kids to help shape their future before it becomes their past.

There are countless ways we hear, "But I turned out fine."

"I never wore a seatbelt and it never hurt me."

"I drank as a teenager and my brain wasn't damaged."

"My grandma smoked from the time she was 12 and died in her 90s — from old age!"

The "I turned out just fine" argument is popular. It means that based on our personal experience, we know what works and what doesn't. There are fatal flaws in this argument, such as generalizing based on data from one person (you), personal biases ("I was spanked and turned out fine, so spanking can be used on anyone"), dismissing research-based evidence and finally… maybe we're not as "fine" as we think we are. Let's not make some of the same mistakes of our parents' generation. Let's use data, let's be informed and let's make sure our kids turn out fine.

Knowing When to Step In or Step Back: The Costs and Benefits of Helicopter versus Free Range Parenting

A *helicopter parent* is defined as a parent who takes an overprotective or excessive interest in the life of their child or children. No doubt there have been helicopter parents years before the term was coined; however, it is not always in the best interest of our children to hover. We're finding more and more young adults who never learned the independent skills necessary to survive and thrive on their own. Now more than in previous generations, there have never been so many reasons for children to learn how to be independent. There are more distractions, obligations, demands, and greater requirements needed to be successful as compared to years past. A supervisor once told me that she believed our role as parents is to "raise our children to be able to survive on their own." To take that a step further, we can raise our children to become empowered instead of enabled.

Maybe we do need to hover? Maybe the world is more dangerous and it's our job to always protect our children and step in until we can't anymore? Before we answer those questions, let's look at some data from the Center for Disease Controls. Based on the statistics, children have never been safer than ever when compared to mortality rates over the last one-hundred and forty years. Statistics also show that the leading causes of death for children are accidents, illnesses, homicide and suicide and these numbers are still very low. As a parent, I completely understand how paralyzing thoughts about something bad happening to your child can be, so it is natural for us to want to protect them.

So back to the question, is it better to step in or step back? Well, it depends on several key factors such as age, maturity, developmental abilities and specificity of the occurrence in which you are deciding to bulldoze your way through or let them figure it out on their own. If the ultimate goal is to instill all the skills necessary in your child in order to survive and thrive, you'll always want to make sure that your child is learning something during each challenge.

Here are some ideas to keep in mind when your instinct may be to swoop in:

1. Keep Your Eyes on the Prize.

For any problem your child has, the ultimate goal should be for them to know how to solve it. From tying their shoes and making a sandwich to waking up on time and emailing their teachers, we should always remind ourselves that children should be learning how to deal with life's problems on their own.

2. Know When to Jump In.

There will be times when you need to help your children. Knowing when will be the difference between being a helicopter parent and a supportive parent.

Examples of times when parents may want to be more closely involved are safety issues (i.e., physical and mental health, dangerous behaviors, etc.), problems that they've tried to solve on their own but keep getting worse (i.e., bullying), or when the problem is out of the child's control (i.e., learning disability or physical ailment).

3. Birds of a Feather Flock Together.

Many parents unconsciously parent similarly to the parents with whom they spend most of their time. If you are usually with parents who do more hovering, there is a greater chance that you will take on some of those behaviors. If you are aware that this is happening, remind yourself of step 1 (see above).

4. Be Consistent.

When our children are learning to be independent, they will have a hard time self-monitoring themselves. Ask any parent who allows their child to play Fortnite. If all children went to sleep when they were tired and studied when they had a test, I'd be out of a job. Whatever your rules are, stay consistent. As your children get older, you can be more flexible with your rules, allowing them to build their own independence and ability to learn from their mistakes.

When it comes to helicopter parenting, we've all been guilty of hovering at some point in our children's lives. Helicopter parenting is the outcome of increased anxiety and environmental stressors. Instead of rushing in to help because "they might fail," we can learn to take a step back and start thinking, "Maybe failing is how they'll learn."

When Parents Can't Agree: How Compromising and Testing Hypotheses Can Reduce Parental Dissent

One of the major factors in reasons for divorce has to do with conflicts over parenting styles.

Most future parents do not discuss every potential situation and decision to be made once they have children. In fact, it is not until the area of dissent arises that parents realize they are not on the same page. If research has shown us anything over the last fifty years, it's that consistency in expectations, actions and reactions is one of the best predictors of children's behavioral, emotional and academic functioning.

One of the most debated topics stems from consequences and discipline. More often than not one parent tends to be more permissive while the other one is more strict. This also encompasses areas such as screen time, academic expectations, chores and responsibilities, spending habits, routines and schedules. Because many parents have been raised differently themselves, they are bringing their own experiences from their environments, cultures and time periods (Baby

Boomers, Gen X, Millennials, etc.) that shape their own parenting styles. While this may create disagreements in viewpoints, it doesn't have to lead to chronic fights about how to parent your children.

Here are some techniques you can use when you and your partner are not on the same page:

1. Compromise.

This sounds easier than it is. Compromising is difficult if you each have very black-and-white views about certain rules and expectations. Social media is a good example in which one parent might think the child shouldn't have any accounts while the other parent thinks some social media use may add to their social life. Think of factors such as the risk versus reward of the behavior, the ultimate goal for the child, safety applications you can put in place, and how finding a common ground is a great way to model compromise with your child.

2. Discuss in private.

While it is not always possible to predict when you and your partner may disagree over something your child wants or needs, it is always better to disagree in private. If your partner says "yes" or "no" to something and your initial reaction is to argue, ask to go somewhere in private. You can even tell your child that their parents need to talk about this more before any final answer is given. If you can't find privacy, make time later in the day in which you can not only start to communicate, but have the time to reduce any intense emotions.

3. Test each hypothesis.

Sometimes, parents will disagree about a topic with little wiggle room for compromise.

One example can be if a child has been recommended to begin a trial of medication for a recent diagnosis of ADHD or anxiety. There are many parents who are completely against medicating a child, fearing potential side effects, while others view medication as a tool to help their child reduce their suffering and get more out of life. Talk with another professional and decide how you can test each hypothesis by collecting data and analyzing the cost versus the benefit.

4. Think of the big picture.

When disagreeing over specific rules and expectations, always keep in mind what the future goal is for your child. If it is something like sleeping with their phone in their bedroom, discuss how learning how to do this will either benefit or hurt them when they begin living on their own. Another example may be how much freedom to give to your child with the purpose of them learning how to self-monitor and learn from their own decisions and consequences.

It is an unrealistic expectation to think you and your partner will agree on everything. In fact, some flexibility is good in that it teaches your child how to compromise and think more critically about their own behaviors and decision-making. Parenting is stressful enough, so try to reduce some of the unnecessary stress by practicing taking space, communication and compromise.

"I Don't Want To Grow Up" When Children and Teenagers Believe Adult is 4-Letter Word

More and more teenagers have struggled with the idea of becoming "adults." The word 'adults' is put in quotes because while the definition of an adult is a person who can take care of themselves, is over the age of eighteen and recognized by most states as one who can make decisions regarding their own lives, many young adults are poorly prepared or apprehensive about one if not all of these responsibilities. There are exceptions, but one thing is clear, our job as parents is to raise our children to be self-reliant and independent. While most parents want their children to not only survive, but thrive, it's technically not our job to ensure our children succeed. However, I do believe it is our duty to instill within them the necessary skills to reach their full potential.

When teenagers are asked to describe what it means to be an adult, most say that when you become an adult, you don't have as much fun, are expected to act like you always know what you are doing and have more impactful consequences for behaviors. No wonder children and teens are scared of growing up; it sounds terrifying! Here's the good news. It doesn't have to be. We as parents can assure them that while they may not continue to play video games or binge shows for eight straight hours, they can still have fun....it just might change as they become older. For some, it remains the same but with better boundaries and limits. Here are some great tips if you work with or have apprehensive future adults:

1. Address Specific Worries.

Bills, signing leases, investing, calling customer service, etc. aren't as complicated as children may think. Show them specifically how to pay bills online or how to make sure they are making the most practical choices for big-money purchases (think of using Consumer Reports or the Better Business Bureau). Also ensure them that they've learned complicated things before and thought it was going to be harder than it was (like algebra!).

2. Practical Solutions.

Let's say some of their fears come true. Help them solve problems by using practical and realistic solutions. One example might be if they aren't able to land a job right away and pay for rent. Some solutions may be having roommates, living at home until they save up enough money, or taking on side jobs to make some extra money. If they worry about choosing the right college or secondary education, reassure them that the worst thing that can happen is that they may have to transfer to a different one. Still a little stressful, but not the end of the world.

3. Practice, practice, practice.

There's a reason that generations of children had responsibilities like doing chores or taking care of younger siblings. Sure, it was helpful to their parents, but it also prepared them for their future and instilled a sense of confidence and responsibility. Children as young as five can take care of putting away their belongings or putting their plates away after dinner. As children become teenagers, you can slowly introduce new responsibilities such as cooking, putting away laundry, or saving money.

4. Stress Tolerance.

One of the best ways of becoming a functional adult

(making decisions based on rationale and not emotion, their future as well as their present) is to learn how to identify and cope with stress. Don't be afraid to model coping skills when you are stressed, but make sure to keep them age-appropriate. One example might be if an unexpected expense arises and you're worried about money. Use phrases such as, "I know we're not going to lose our house, but I'm feeling nervous and am going to take a little me time to calm myself down," or "This is a little stressful, but I'm going to wait a day or two to let my brain calm down before I make any big decisions." You can begin teaching children as young as when they are in preschool to manage their own stress by identifying their triggers, building coping skills, and learning how to communicate what they feel and need.

With each generation, it appears that children and teenagers are having more and more difficulty with the idea of becoming adults. There are many factors contributing to their maturational reluctance (social media, global catastrophes, increased school pressure), but like I heard on a sports radio show once, "Father time is undefeated." No matter what, they will become adults…at least in the eyes of the government. Instead of coddling them or minimizing their worries, help them shift their mindset while also reassuring them that it's not as hard as they perceive it to be.

SOCIAL/EMOTIONAL FUNCTIONING

Mental Health 101: Strategies to Promote Mental Wellness in Children and Teens

According to the most up-to-date research, there has been a rise in childhood and teen anxiety, depression and suicide over the past 20 years. This is a scary trend and one that greatly impacts how we parent and teach our children. Luckily, this rise has also led to an increase in mental health awareness and activism. Schools are starting to implement mental health curriculum in the form of mindfulness practice, mental health first aid, teaching of warning signs and symptoms of emotional distress and suicide prevention. However, resources are working unilaterally instead of collaboratively which has led to inconsistency and delays in prevention and treatment.

When looking at mental health through a medical lens, emphasis should be placed on having a team of experts whose main goal is to do what is best for the child.

If we look at promoting physical well-being, it's pretty well documented that if you exercise, eat and sleep well, avoid drug and alcohol use and minimize stress as best as you can, you'll increase your chances of remaining pretty healthy. We can look at emotional well-being through a similar lens and until there is a joint effort between schools, mental health professionals and parents, we will need to make sure we do our part at home to promote and model psychological well-being.

Here are some important ways to promote mental health in your children:

1. Teach Your Children How to Understand, Manage and Express Their Feelings.

Just like we teach reading and writing, we can teach children that feelings are like clouds, they are normal, vary in strength and duration and always go away. Most parents' goal for their children is to be happy, but happiness is a feeling and feelings don't last forever. Teach this to your children. Teach them that there are healthy ways to manage and express negative and positive feelings. You can begin talking to children as young as two about how they feel while also validating and comforting.

("You're really upset. It's upsetting when you don't get to keep playing.")

2. Allow Failure While Promoting Growth.

Your child will lose at something... and that is okay. There is no better way to learn how to handle disappointment and frustration than practicing dealing with disappointment and frustration. Use growth mindset language such as "You're not able to get an A yet" or "You're still working on your multiplication facts." Failure will eventually lead to perseverance which will oftentimes lead to healthy self-esteem.

3. Create Balance.

It is no secret that children are more overscheduled than at any other time in human history. Children who have too many obligations and not enough "downtime" often report more feelings of stress and anxiety. Prioritize with your child what is important to them and ensure there is time to relax, socialize and spend time with the family.

4. Diet, Exercise and Sleep.

This may be the most obvious way to promote physical health but it is probably the hardest and most neglected way to promote psychological health as well. More and more research is showing that children who have healthy diets (balanced), get at least an hour of physical activity a day and sleep more than 7-9 hours each night report less feelings of stress and anxiety compared to those who do not follow one or all of these recommendations. You can model these behaviors and start as young as preschool. Family bike rides, fun dinner routines (meatless Monday, Salmon Saturday) and healthy sleep habits (no electronics one hour before bed) are great ways to start.

Like most diseases, it is always easier to prevent a problem than treat it. Increased academic demands, isolationism among children and teens, overscheduling and environmental stressors are all impacting our children's mental health. These factors will likely be around for the near future, which is why it is important to teach our children how to cope with them. So when we're talking about children's health, let's make sure this includes their mental health as well.

How Teaching Our Children How to Cope with Their Emotions Just Might Save Their Lives

"I wish I was dead!"

"You ruined my life!!"

"I hate you!"

For any parent who has heard their child make one of these statements or a barrage of other emotionally charged statements, it is both heartbreaking and scary. Recent research has shown that our children are experiencing more stress, anxiety, and depression than past generations and that factors that are contributing to this sharp rise are not going away any time soon (i.e., social media, increased isolation, high-stakes testing, etc.). Because it is almost impossible to control every factor creating increased distress, we can help our children by teaching them about their emotions and how to cope with them in healthy and safe ways. Moreover, by modeling these skills and creating an open dialogue from an early age, you can increase your child's feelings of self-worth, perseverance and emotional well-being into adulthood.

1. Feelings are normal.

Too many times, we want to tell our children, "Don't be sad" or "You have nothing to be nervous about." This often doesn't work and indirectly lets them know that feelings are either good or bad, normal or abnormal, or acceptable or unacceptable. Let's be clear.

There are no good or bad feelings, just feelings. Try using phrases such as "That's a pretty normal feeling to have right now," or "I bet anyone else would be sad if that happened to them too." What is not as common are specific thoughts and behaviors that accompany feelings that include

2. Feelings are like clouds.

This is one of my favorite analogies, even for older kids. Feelings are like clouds. Some are dark, while others are light. Some hang around while others move quickly. Some are big and heavy, while others are light and fluffy. But no matter how they look or feel, they always go away. This is a great way to teach children how to accept their feelings, let them experience them and allow them to naturally move on.

3. We don't have to live in our feelings or thoughts.

Kids' minds are usually blown when you teach them that feelings and thoughts are not tangible or real. Don't get me wrong, they are very real because they occur and shape our reality and self-talk; however, you can't see them, you can't touch them and there is no evidence of them after their gone... see, mind blown! Once children learn that these thoughts are driven by strong emotions like anger, frustration, or embarrassment and that they are just noise due to strong emotions, they can learn how to focus on something else until that feeling passes. Below are apps, websites, and resources to help children learn to focus on the present environment rather than their thoughts until their feelings pass.

4. We can always get better.

Teach children that, like many other things they need to practice to get better at (think sports, reading, math, gaming, etc.), they can improve their abilities to cope with negative feelings and learn to turn down the volume on those negative thoughts. Do some of these activities as a family, and don't wait until everyone is stressed. If you practice these skills when calm, you increase your chances of using them effectively when under duress.

You can't turn on the news or read social media without seeing articles on teen suicide, high levels of anxiety and depression in children, or students burning out because of increased pressure and decreased connection with family and peers. Not to sound like an alarmist (too late?), but if we don't begin teaching our children from a young age how to handle what is to come, they run the risk of developing unhealthy coping skills. Think 6 straight hours alone in a room with nothing but YouTube and Fortnite. While a little technology can be a nice distraction, overdoing it may lead to increased anxiety and depression while missing out on meaningful experiences. So remember when you get angry at your child for waiting last minute to do homework because they were on their phones... your feelings are like clouds.

Go Play! The Importance of Play for Children and Adults

As I sit watching my son and his friend at a trampoline park, I can't help but think that this is no longer the norm (free and unstructured play, that is...well, not free). As a Gen X-er, I often find myself lamenting over the slow decline of "hanging out." Research has shown that unstructured play has been on the decline for the past fifty years. There are multiple factors causing this steady recession, including increased academic demands, technological advancements (online gaming, streaming videos and social media) and helicopter or hovering parenting styles.

Fortunately, most infants and toddlers are given plenty of opportunities to play in daycare or preschool, but as children enter elementary and middle school, free play often has to be coordinated like it's a formal event.

Many adults think that children are busier with activities of greater importance. However, scientists have learned that free play isn't just something children like to do—it's something they need to do. Play keeps children physically active, all the more important at a time when roughly 20% of American children are obese—more than triple the percentage from the more

play-friendly 1970s. (Early activity habits matter—a 2005 study in the *American Journal of Preventive Medicine* found that the most active 9-to-18-year-olds remained the most active later in life.) Play also provides exercise for their problem-solving and their creativity. More than anything else, play teaches children how to work together and, at the same time, how to be alone. It teaches them how to be human. https://time.com/4928925/secret-power-play/

A paradigm shift to a more play-friendly environment will take individual and collective effort. Here are some helpful tips to ensure that play becomes a daily habit in your child's (even your own) life:

1. Facilitate.

When children communicate with each other on their devices, not all do so with the purpose of getting together. You will likely have to get in touch with other parents to coordinate times your children can hang out. You might also have to go out of your way by acting as the chauffeur or ATM machine but it will always be worth it in the long run.

2. Build Relationships with Other Parents.

Many parents are convinced that if their children leave the house, they will get kidnapped, raped, hurt, abused or killed. Parents have told me for years that they trust their children, they just don't trust anyone else. Ergo, get other parents to trust you. Get to know the parents well enough when your children are young so that when they grow older and want to have sleepovers or bike back and forth from each others' houses, those parents feel more comfortable.

3. Set Play Times.

Parents can set specific play time for children as young as 1-2 years old. Set limits on technology and give the option instead of playing alone or with a parent(s) or sibling(s). Once children enter middle school, they seem to be drawn to their rooms like middle school girls to Sephora. Start these routines early and follow them yourselves. It is also a good idea to have things for them to do if they are not allowed to use technology or to stay in their rooms for a few hours. Board games, exploring new areas in the city, going to friends' houses, or even hanging out at the mall can all be options for children and teens.

4. Play is not just for Kids.

Adults can model play by having their own leisurely activities. We can go to trivia nights with friends, learn a new instrument, play sports, have game nights, or even build Legos (I'm partial to the Lord of the Rings sets myself). By setting aside time to engage in fun activities, you are modeling the importance of setting boundaries between work and play.

Play has been a crucial part of child development for thousands of years. Research has shown that play can be just as important, if not more, than any kind of test prep frequently taking the place of recess in schools. Unfortunately, the days when kids got on their bikes and came back before dark are almost extinct. However, with a little bit of work, we can ensure that all children get opportunities to "Go Play!"

Just Wait: How Delaying Gratification Might be the Most Important Skill You Teach Your Children

There is a famous experiment conducted with children in the 1960s and early 1970s at Stanford University in which a child was offered a choice between one small reward provided immediately or two small rewards if they waited for a short period, approximately 15 minutes, during which the tester left the room and then returned. (The reward was sometimes a marshmallow, but often a cookie or a pretzel). In follow-up studies, the researchers found that children who were able to wait longer for the preferred rewards tended to have better life outcomes, as measured by SAT scores, educational attainment, body mass index (BMI), and other life measures.

Many children (and adults as well) are not used to waiting to get what they want. That is probably why this generation is stereotyped as needing instant gratification. Children no longer have to wait until next week for their favorite show's next episode or the morning paper to find out the box score for a late basketball game. Don't even bother asking a child or teenager what an encyclopedia or card catalog is! At the cost of sounding like a dinosaur (too late), kids don't know how easy they have it... and that is part of the problem. We are taking away opportunities for children to wait or work for things. In the experiment listed above, they were better able to predict a child's future just based on their ability to wait for a greater reward. Here are some ways at home to help children learn to delay their gratification:

1. Just wait one more minute.

You can start small by having your children wait an extra minute to get their iPad, start eating dessert, leave the dinner table, etc. This can eventually increase to two or five minutes. The whole point is your child is practicing being "uncomfortable" or "bored" and not giving into their initial impulse.

2. Change the topic.

Research found that talking more about the reward they are waiting for made it harder for kids to wait for it. Instead, talk about something totally different. For example, if they are waiting to watch Netflix, don't talk about what show they are watching. Instead, ask about specific details of their day or if they are looking forward to anything the family is doing over the next few weeks.

3. Distraction.

This works well with younger children. If they are begging for the iPad, do something with them that is engaging and fun, such as singing songs they enjoy, going on a nature or exploration walk, playing I Spy or a word game, etc.

4. Allowance.

Allowance is a great way to start teaching children how to wait to get what they want. If they have to save up for something they want (not need), they will appreciate it more when they buy it. It will also teach them the value of money, how to avoid impulse buying as well as responsibility and budgeting.

Studies show that delayed gratification is one of the most effective personal traits of successful people. People who learn how to manage their need to be satisfied at the moment thrive more in their careers, relationships, health, and finances than people who give in to it. It is harder now more than ever to help children learn how to delay getting what they want with advanced technology, globalization and social media, which is why it is more important than ever to start practicing as soon as you can.

There's No Crying In Childhood?

While observing a child and her mother nearby, I overheard the following conversation:

Parent: "So the teacher told me you were crying today."

Child: "Yeah, I got scared when it started thundering."

Parent: "You have to be brave and not cry."

Child: "I tried but I couldn't help it!"

So the question is, what's wrong with crying? Isn't it natural for someone to cry when they are upset, especially a child? Science has actually shown that crying releases a stress hormone, leading to relaxation and emotional regulation. It appears that many parents have taken the opinion that crying is either embarrassing for them as a parent, a sign of weakness, or an opportunity to rescue their child and remove any unpleasantness in their life.

If you grew up in previous generations, you've probably heard your own parents say things like, "I'll give you something to cry about" or "Don't be a baby!" If we unpack the meaning behind these reactions, it often leads to parents experiencing feelings of guilt, inadequacy and loss. Loss of the opportunity to express themselves in a world in which boys were told (overtly or passive-aggressively) that boys are supposed to be tough and not cry. Fast forward to today where the pendulum has swung to parents becoming overly sensitive to their children's discomfort. This may lead to them inadvertently stunting their children's abilities to self-soothe, leading to a greater sense of independent emotional regulation.

So next time your child begins to cry, remind yourself of the following:

1. Healthy Coping Skills.

If you think of all of the ways to cope with sadness, anger, frustration, etc., crying is one of the safest and healthiest. When denied the opportunity to cry, children can start developing maladaptive coping skills such as violence toward themselves or others, aggression and/or negative self-talk.

2. Discomfort is Good.

How are kids supposed to develop healthy coping skills unless given the opportunity to use them? In the age of helicopter parenting and increased fear and anxiety, it is more important than ever to teach children that negative emotions are just as important as positive emotions and by learning to cope with them early in life, you will become a pro when faced with uncomfortable feelings later in life.

3. A Good Lesson for Adults as Well.

We are all doing our best as parents and caregivers. It's unfortunate that society has those that judge us without knowing our story. Remind yourself that letting your child cry DOES NOT make you a bad parent. The intent of letting your child cry should always be to teach and allow healthy development. We can let ourselves cry as well rather than suppressing it as a model for them to understand that crying is a normal response to certain feelings.

4. Gender Correlation.

It's hard to ignore the correlation between mass shootings and white male perpetrators. I know it is a bit of a stretch, but I'm curious how many of these mass shooters or any shooters were not allowed to develop healthy coping skills as children, which developed into unchecked aggression as adults. The gender bias still remains true to this day that boys should be tough and tough means not crying.

It appears that adults are more triggered now than in past generations by their children crying. While telling children they shouldn't cry, or that (boys, teenagers, big kids, etc.) don't cry is also not okay, we also shouldn't do everything in our power to prevent children from crying or jumping through hoops to get them to stop. From someone who has cried plenty of times in his adult life, crying can be a healthy coping skill that children should be taught is completely normal. In simple terms, if you're happy, you smile, and if you're sad, you cry.

Preventing Mental Illness in Children

Parents can have a tough time explaining what a mental health professional does and why they might have to see one. Many times the therapist has to re-explain the purpose of therapy, but there should be a universal mindset when it comes to children. Psychologists should focus on being preventionists instead of just interventionists. In most fields of psychology, we usually see patients and/or children when there is a problem. Rarely do people think of a visit to a psychologist as a preventative measure. By equating going to the therapist with seeing any other medical specialist, we can help prevent severe mental illness, self-harm and addiction.

Prevention is almost always easier and more effective than interventions. Think of cancer. It's much easier (and cheaper) to prevent cancer than to treat it. The same goes for anxiety, depression, post-traumatic stress and so on. If we focus enough energy and effort on children, we can decrease their chances of later being diagnosed with one or more of these mental illnesses. Here are a few tips for focusing on prevention rather than reaction:

1. Start healthy habits early.

If you have young children, begin building a balanced routine of alone and social time, structured and unstructured activities, work and playtime and active and relaxation time.

If your children are older, it is never too late to start promoting a balanced lifestyle that they will take with them into adulthood.

2. Talk about feelings.

As cliche as it may be, talking about feelings can help save lives. Suicide still kills about

40,000 - 50,000 people each year and is the 2nd leading cause of death in teens and young adults. By normalizing and talking about feelings from a young age, you help teach children that most feelings are normal. That it is ok to feel sad, nervous, scared, angry, embarrassed and annoyed and that these feelings don't last forever. That it is good to talk about them because these feelings might be causing problems that require additional support.

3. Let them feel

It is no surprise that the reason many younger generations are labeled as entitled is that their parents do not allow them to fail or experience any negativity long enough for them to learn how to cope properly. Letting kids feel the full array of negative emotions without "rescuing" them gives them opportunities to increase the tools in their coping skills toolbox for the rest of their lives.

4. Connection and support.

The saying "it takes a village" is particularly pertinent, now more than ever. Humans have evolved as social creatures. Our brains crave physical, emotional and social connections with other humans. Research has shown that the more deep connections people have, the lower their chances of experiencing severe mental illness, self-harm or suicide.

Ensure your children have these connections with family, peers, teachers, coaches, etc. to provide social nourishment.

While many people are focusing on physical health, we should equally focus on the mental well being of ourselves and our children. Stressful events often come with spikes in severe emotional impairment, desperation and loneliness. While there are certain factors we don't have as much control over, like the economy or epidemics, we can prioritize our children's abilities to build healthy habits.

If you know someone who needs help, please reach out to any of the national or local organizations that provide help.

National Suicide Prevention Hotline: 1-800-273-8255 or text "home" to 741741 to connect with a crisis counselor

National Alliance on Mental Illness: 1-800-950-NAMI

Mental Health America: 1-800-969-6642

How To Administer a Mental Health Check-up

While most parents are able to determine if their children or loved ones need medical attention, knowing if they require mental health intervention is more difficult to determine. There is no thermometer that reads a child's emotional functioning. However, with the right set of tools, you can determine if your child needs help from a mental health professional.

Parents often know their children best and know when something looks or sounds wrong. When doctors administer a medical check-up, they have a baseline they use to determine if there needs to be further evaluation or intervention. We have the same baseline when it comes to our children's behaviors, emotional reactions and social interactions. The purpose of learning how to determine if your child needs help is to prevent things from getting any worse.

Here are some simple steps when administering a mental health check-up:

1. Use your eyes and ears.

The first thing to do when being an observer is to use your eyes and ears. Do you see any differences in your child's behaviors? Do you hear changes in voice tone, repeated phrases, or reactions to stressors that sound different than before? Look for changes in eating, sleeping and energy levels, as well as changes in hobbies, interests and time with peers.

2. Ask, don't tell.

More often than not, people's mental health is a private matter, especially for children (think of angst-ridden teens). You can start by asking them basic questions about how they feel, if they are stressed about anything or if they need anything from you. If they answer no, that's when you can report to them what you've observed (from step 1). Try saying something like, "I can see that you have been going to sleep later," or "Your voice is telling me that you're feeling annoyed or frustrated about something."

3. Tools in their toolbox:

You finally want to find out how they cope with any negative emotions or stressors they are experiencing. Connect their coping skills and emotions by saying things like, "It looks like you prefer to be alone when you are in a bad mood" or "So watching YouTube helps you turn your brain off." Sharing your own coping skills can also help normalize the different ways they deal with their own emotions.

4. Determining the next step:

If you have learned during the mental health check-up that your child or loved one is having severe symptoms of emotional distress, you should call a mental health professional immediately (i.e., self-harm, suicidal or homicidal thoughts, etc.). More often you will discover mild to moderate symptoms, such as changes in mood or behavior due to new or prolonged stressors (like the current quarantine or isolation). If your children or loved ones are coping by using non-threatening coping skills, you'd want to encourage them not to become too reliant on one strategy (i.e., gaming, YouTube, social media) and should have lots of "tools in their coping toolbox." There are too many to name but during times when they are off from school, you'd want to encourage strategies that provide opportunities they cannot get by staying indoors all day, such as going for a bike ride/walk/hike, having a group chat through video conferencing, finding things in the home to donate to a local shelter or playing board games with the family.

Hopefully, in the near future, a mental health check-up is just as commonplace as a medical check-up. Until then, parents and teachers will often be the first line of defense in assessing children's mental health status. So let's make sure we're all aware of the signs, know how to gather more information and when to reach out for help.

Below are some important phone numbers and website:

- National Suicide Prevention Hotline: 1-800-273-8255
- National Alliance on Mental Illness: www.nami.org

National Institute of Mental Health: www.nimh.nih.gov/index.shtml

Learning to Live With Anxiety (Not Cure It)

Without anxiety, humans would have gone extinct years ago. It has kept us safe, alerted us to danger and provided us with an intrinsic warning system that unfortunately has become overactive in the past few generations. To describe it simply, anxiety is a physical reaction to a potential threat (think of a shark swimming at you in open waters). When anxious, our bodies get ready to fight, flee or freeze. Like the shark example, this is great when there is real danger because all of our body's resources kick into gear. Our blood travels to our limbs so we can run away or fight. Our pupils dilate so we can focus better. Breathing becomes shallow, which activates the sympathetic nervous system, getting the body ready for action. All great things, unless this is a false alarm (no real impending threat to our safety).

Many practitioners and anxious children look at anxiety as a disease to be eradicated, like cancer. This sets up many children for an unreasonable expectation, which oftentimes leads to greater anxiety and frustration. Instead, we can teach our children to learn how to live with and even thrive with anxiety. It helps to think of anxiety as a roommate that can be annoying or even a nightmare at times, but one that we need to help pay the rent.

Here are some helpful tips for helping your children (and yourself) learn to live with rather than cure their anxiety:

1. Normalize and Educate.

When we first teach children that anxiety is a normal emotion, like all other emotions, it reduces the stress and shock when it appears. Teach them that anxiety can fluctuate in duration and intensity and always go away. This last part is the most important and helpful for children. Even though it may feel like it will never end, it always does.

2. Teach real-life strategies for all kinds of settings.

Most children will want to use the same strategies to cope with anxiety, but you can't start watching videos in the middle of class or during a test. Think of strategies as tools in a toolbox. Watching videos may help, but time and place matter. Strategies can include deep breathing, mindful practices, talking to a trusted friend or adult and even distractions until the feeling begins to dissipate.

3. Prepare.

You can guarantee that you or your child(ren) will experience anxiety at some point in the near future. By knowing it will happen, we can prepare for when it does. For example, if you know your child is anxious before flying, implement specific strategies to use before and during the flight (i.e., most enjoyable activities, tasks that take lots of attention and problem-solving, mindful distractions, etc.). Are new situations difficult?

Pair it with something relaxing and focus on how the anxiety is normal and will eventually subside like it always does.

4. Knowing when to get help.

When anxiety persists for months with more anxious than non-anxious days, when it negatively impacts one's life and when activities that were enjoyable become triggers for heightened states of anxiety, are signs that it is time to get help for you or your child.

Think of it as an infection. Doctors always say that if your cough persists for over 7-10 days, go see a professional. Same idea here. It doesn't necessarily mean they need intensive therapy or medicine, it just means that you need to add some members to the team.

Anxiety is a normal part of the human experience. Just like happiness, anger, disgust, sadness and all other emotions, anxiety doesn't have to have a negative connotation attached to it. When children and parents learn to accept it, it will not continue to seem like the big, scary monster waiting in the closet. And if we can learn to not fear it, it will have less and less power and control over children's overall well-being.

It's All In Your Head: Helping Your Children with Anxious Thoughts & Feelings

For anyone who has experienced severe anxiety, you know that it can be crippling and cause just as much distress as physical pain. This holds true for children as well. Children can become even more negatively impacted by their anxiety because they haven't developed the right tools to cope with it yet. When children initially experience severe anxiety, they often become frightened and confused. What is this new feeling? Why is it so bad? Will it ever go away?

Parents and caregivers can begin to teach their children that anxiety is a normal emotion that evolved to keep humans alive (i.e., not petting a poisonous snake or jumping off a cliff). In fact, some anxiety is healthy and necessary. The problem begins when the anxiety becomes too severe and for too long, thus leading to a higher probability of children developing unhealthy coping skills unless we intervene.

Here are some helpful tips to help children better understand and cope with their anxiety:

1. Give them a peek of the man behind the curtain.

We can help children with anxiety by first teaching them what it is, where it comes from and that it can be managed. You can use age-appropriate books or websites to help teach that anxiety is a real, biologically-based occurrence that can be measured and treated. In the long run, this will help children identify it and not be as scared when it occurs.

2. Normalize and validate.

Anxiety shouldn't be thought of as a disease to eradicate but as a normal emotion that comes and goes like all other emotions. By doing so, your child won't be as alarmed when they get anxious but look at it as a symptom of some kind of stressor. Validate their emotions by saying things like, "It's ok to be nervous," "I'll always be here for you," or "You've been this anxious before and remind yourself it always goes away."

3. This too shall pass.

Getting back to the science, remind children that all emotions don't last forever, including the ones that don't feel so good. The human body does not have the energy to sustain severe emotions for too long. By helping children look at negative emotions more like waves that ebb and flow, we can help them ride out the wave by using healthy coping skills. This also provides underlying confidence in their own abilities to cope with anxiety.

4. Teach coping skills.

Coping skills are just that. Skills we use to cope with specific situations or feelings that are unpleasant. Make sure that your children have a full toolbox of skills that can be used in multiple settings. Sometimes the iPad or phone can be helpful, but other times, they may need to go for a walk/break, talk to someone, read or find some other mindful activity that gives their anxious brain time to settle down.

It's no surprise that anxiety rates in children are the highest we've seen since we began measuring it. Society puts more demands, allows for less free time and inundates them with so much information that their brains have become wired in a state of constant hyperarousal. Instead of waiting for a major shift in environmental factors or legislation prioritizing children's mental well-being, let's equip our children with tools they can use for the rest of their lives.

What If? The Two Dirtiest Words in the Anxiety Dictionary

"What if I get a bad grade?" "What if I get sick?" "What if I get anxious?" '*What if*' thinking can lead to some of our most irrational and debilitating fears. If you ask anyone who has had to cope with an anxiety disorder how often they experience "what if" thoughts, they will likely say "all the time." Ironically, what if thinking is based on a future that has not happened yet. And unless you are Nostradamus, you can't predict if your "what if" will come true with 100% accuracy. Children are just as susceptible to this type of thinking error, often called *Fortune Telling*. Because of their more limited experiences and continued brain development, emotional regions of their brains are unreliable data collectors, meaning many of their beliefs are based on feelings and not facts.

One example may be the teenage student who is convinced they are going to fail the upcoming test. If you ask them if they often fail tests, they will most likely say "no." Why is it then they believe they are going to fail the next one? They have no historical data to prove their theory to be likely true. Their belief is often rooted in their anxiety which, unfortunately, is usually much louder in their minds than their more realistic, rational thoughts. Parents will have to help their children during these times of 'What If' thinking to validate their feelings while getting them to recognize several measurable facts.

Here are some ideas of how to help children in the moment of their "what if "thoughts:

1. Help them answer their "what if" thoughts.

Many children get so stuck on the "what if" they are unable to focus on what will actually happen if it actually happens. So, if you get a bad grade, you might have to retake the test or study harder for the next one. If you get sick, we'll go to the doctor, or you might throw up and then feel better. Help them answer the what if by asking them to continue down the path of what will be the most likely outcome.

2. It might be uncomfortable for a little while.

Instead of invalidating their anxious thoughts by saying things like, "You shouldn't worry," or "That'll never happen," try telling them that it might be uncomfortable for a short time. Help them realize that they've been anxious before and have always been able to handle it until it goes

away. Telling your child not to be nervous because their thoughts are irrational is like telling your dog that he doesn't have to bark at the delivery driver because he saw them yesterday.

3. *What if* thinking can just as likely be positive.

Funny how '*what if*' thinking never talks about what if something good happens. What if you get a better grade than you think? What if you don't get sick? When a child is not thinking rationally, it is hard for them to use the more logical centers of their brains. We have to remind them that the chances are that it will not be as bad as they think it will be.

4. Don't hate, validate.

I thought it'd be funny to have a cheesy slogan (very 80s like). But it is very applicable here. We should always validate a person's thoughts and feelings because that is their current reality.

However, we don't have to hate the anxiety. We can look at it as a warning sign. Maybe they are under a lot of stress that is surfacing in other ways. Maybe saying something like, "I know you're super anxious but it's ok. It'll go away soon, so let's do some other things until it does." Or "Those thoughts sound like they can make you very nervous. What do you think we can do to focus on something else for a bit?"

'What if' thinking can turn into a terrible habit for children, but it doesn't mean that we can't help them learn a new way of thinking. Children having supportive people in their lives who validate their feelings while helping them develop better ways of coping with these types of thoughts can hopefully turn those "What ifs" into "So what!"

Helping Children Learn How to Manage Panic Attacks

If you've never experienced a panic attack, consider yourself lucky. For anyone that has never experienced a panic attack, it feels like you're trapped on a horrible ride and you can't get off...and worse yet, you don't know how long the ride will last. Nausea, feeling unreal or not in control of your own body and having a flight or fight response are often a part of the ride. What's worse is that panic can be triggered by anything...or nothing! Sometimes the thought that you might get a panic attack is all it takes. For children, it is frightening and confusing. They might think they are sick or having breathing problems and don't realize that anxiety has a huge impact on our body's physical responses.

Now for some good news. Panic can be managed and, in many cases, prevented. Another positive characteristic of a panic attack is that they can't sustain for too long due to the amount of energy they exhaust. If your child experiences a panic attack, it's helpful to know the following information:

1. Everyone is different.

Some children need to be alone while others need to be around specific people. There are those that need quiet while others need distractions. You can always start by asking your child what they need by giving them two different choices (i.e., Go outside or find a different room where you are, listen to some music or find a quiet space). This can also be used as a preventative measure having a plan for "just in case" (i.e., Before a possible triggering event, come up with a plan like taking a break, going for a walk, having a way to escape, etc.).

2. No pressure.

Children who are experiencing panic are already under enough stress, so don't add any. Reminding them that if you need to turn around, cancel dinner, go home, etc. helps relieve some of the stress. For many, just knowing there is an "escape" is enough to help the panic subside faster thus leading them to feel more empowered.

3. Frustration.

Panic causes a lot of frustration. Children may feel that they are missing out or "ruining" an event or occasion for everyone else. This can lead to feelings of guilt as well.

Because of this, the child may snap at you or sound angry. Just remember, it's nothing personal or disrespectful.

4. Riding the wave.

There's an analogy equating panic to a wave that continuously rises and falls. While children are riding the wave they might do things that appear "weird." Some will pace while others might be on their phones more. Many need a strong distraction. Try not to judge and encourage them to use their strategies until the wave ebbs back into the ocean.

Panic attacks are no joke! Imagine anxiety amped up to an eleven for a short period, then back down to a five, then up again. With the proper mindset, coping skills and practice, children can reduce their frequency and intensity but still need those around them to show understanding and patience.

Is Your Child Socially Anxious or an Introvert?

I'm as extroverted as can be. I have labrador energy when I'm around other people and feel excited by opportunities to socialize with friends, family and interesting acquaintances. But, as a child, my social life was stifled by my need for external approval. I did everything I could to ensure others liked me, I didn't disappoint them nor ruin their good time. This social anxiety sometimes made me come across as shy, even though I was never truly an introvert.

Social anxiety is one of several disorders under the umbrella of anxiety. It's the experience of significant nervousness, fear or apprehension in social situations or when thinking about social situations. This anxiety generally stems from a fear of rejection or negative judgment.

If your child struggles with social anxiety, they may avoid situations, groups or environments – even if they want to join – because they're worried about how they'll be received. As a result, your child may get quiet or withdrawn. But this isn't because they don't desire the company of others. In fact, your child may crave socializing and wish they had more friends, but their social anxiety pushes them to avoid hanging out with classmates or teammates, meeting new people or speaking up around others.

Introverts, on the other hand, are those who regain their mental and emotional (and sometimes physical) energy when they're alone. They may prefer alone time over social engagement because they find socializing tiring.

If your child is a natural introvert, they may stay quiet in social situations because being "on" drains their mental and emotional battery. Like those with social anxiety, your introvert child may decide to stay in their room instead of going to a casual get-together with classmates. They may need some alone time after you pick them up from a birthday party.

Since many kids rely on social media interactions instead of face-to-face engagement, fewer children have enough opportunities to hone their social muscles in real-world settings and situations. As a result, parents, teachers and child psychologists like me are seeing an increase in social anxiety in children and teens.

Let's figure out what's really happening with your child.

Before you take your child or teen to therapy for matters related to social avoidance (e.g., gaming all day, not leaving their room, little to no plans with peers, etc.), gather more information to determine if your child is more of an introvert or a socially anxious kid.

1. The reason:

If your child shares that they don't want to go to a birthday party, for instance, because afterwards they'll be tired the rest of the day, and all the noise and chaos is a bit overwhelming, that is typical of a child with introverted tendencies. If they don't want to go to the party because they're worried about embarrassing themselves, having no one to talk to and feeling left out, that's more common in a child with traits of social anxiety.

2. Symptoms:

Common symptoms of social anxiety include nausea/stomachache, dizziness, rapid heartbeat/sweating and other physical signs of anxiety when thinking about, preparing for and/or during social engagements. A child with social anxiety might begin showing these symptoms up to several days before an anxiety-provoking event. Introverted children and teens, however, don't usually experience these symptoms in relation to socializing.

3. Enjoyment or avoidance:

Introverts truly enjoy their alone time. They experience it as a practice of self-care and a time when they can engage in whatever activity they want without having to negotiate or compromise with others.

When alone, introverted children don't feel pressured to make others laugh or go along with activities they're not interested in. On the other hand, socially anxious children and teens choose to avoid social situations to feel safe, to calm themselves and to avoid becoming more anxious in front of others. They may choose to stay home while also feeling left out and frustrated that they're not part of the fun.

4. Friends or fails:

Introverted children and teens are interested in building and maintaining relationships with others on their own terms and engaging socially when they feel up to it. Meanwhile, socially anxious people are often concerned about failing in relationships. Examples of socially anxious thinking include being overly concerned that they'll do something embarrassing, others will think they're "weird" as well as not knowing how others perceive them.

Both introverts and extroverts can experience social anxiety.

Like many other personality traits, sociability is a spectrum – from the shy kid in the back of the classroom to the class clown and the social butterfly. Some children with social anxiety overcome it and come out of their shells when spending time with close friends and family, around whom they feel safe and not judged. Social anxiety is a problem when it overrides your child's desire to engage in social activities they actually want to participate in.

If you and your child figure out that they're experiencing unwanted thoughts and feelings associated with social anxiety, individual and group therapy may be effective. If you're unsure where to begin, ask your child's school counselor/advisor and your friends about local social skills groups and therapists who specialize in treating social anxiety in pediatric patients.

ADHD, Anxiety or Both?

ADHD and anxiety disorders are some of the most commonly diagnosed disorders in children and teens. Let's start with a few numbers. About 10% of children are diagnosed with ADHD. Of those 10%, about 1/3 are also diagnosed with an anxiety disorder. Now, about 7% of children are diagnosed with an anxiety disorder and of those 7%, about a quarter of them also meet the criteria for ADHD. Confusing, I know. What it boils down to is that it gets complicated when determining if a child has ADHD, an anxiety disorder or both. This is important because once we know the primary cause of any maladaptive or unhealthy behavior, we can more effectively treat it.

The main difference between ADHD and anxiety ultimately comes down to whether or not the individual is not focused because of fearful, apprehensive thoughts, or because of being easily distracted even though their mind is calm. If you've ever been anxious or experienced panic-like symptoms, you know only too well how difficult concentrating can be. Now imagine a child trying this without a fully formed frontal lobe, poor coping skills and automatic negative thoughts interfering with their thinking and performance.

Here are some tips to find the correct diagnosis and eventually help your child improve their coping skills:

1. Find a specialist.

This sounds simple, but you'll want to find someone who specializes in both attention and anxiety disorders, such as a pediatric psychiatrist or licensed school or clinical psychologist. Make sure you ask if they have specific training with regard to the assessment of ADHD and anxiety disorders. While many pediatricians have some training with ADHD, most do not have the proper background with mood disorders (i.e., anxiety, depression, bipolar, etc).

2. Prioritize what to address first.

Ranking problematic behavior can be very helpful when planning and prioritizing what is impacting your child's functioning the most. Try asking which symptoms are causing the most stress/trouble in school and/or home. You can rank them numerically or by intensity (1 - negative thoughts, 2 - difficulty getting started on tasks, 3 - staying focused).

3. Help develop better strategies.

If you determine that the greatest dysfunctional behavior is getting started on tasks, start to develop strategies with your child to help get started. Finding the right environment (not their bed), the right time (not at bedtime) and with whom to work can lead to greater efficiency. Try creating a short work interval before they can stop and get some feedback (i.e., "Just do the first two problems. I'll be here in the kitchen starting dinner. When you get the first two done, stop and show me.") You can also try to have them get started in school or on the bus to help with initiation.

4. More Intensive Interventions.

Think of interventions as layers, with each layer becoming slightly more intensive. The first layer may not work (such as strategies in #3), which means you may need something requiring more effort, like a school-home collaboration plan or a specific reward system. If this layer of support doesn't work, you may want to talk to specialists about the types of therapy they can offer. While medication can help children with ADHD, anxiety disorders or both, they may also need additional support and/or therapy, including cognitive-behavioral, family therapy or more environmental changes (i.e., sleep, diet, exercise).

Getting a correct diagnosis of ADHD or anxiety will likely lead to more targeted and individualized interventions. Don't get too caught up in labels, but do ask what will help your child improve their ways of coping with symptoms. We should view and treat these types of disorders similar to the way we view and treat any other medical issue... with data, research and collaboration.

Your Child Is Diagnosed with Autism ...
Now What?

Based on the odds, you know or love someone with autism. Your child may be on the autism spectrum.

Not so long ago, this diagnosis meant an arduous and limited path forward. These days, with the right treatment and support, children and adults with autism spectrum disorder can lead a happy and fulfilling life.

More young adults are now being recognized as falling on the autism spectrum. This might be due to more effective diagnostic practices or the effects of socio-environmental factors. If your child is on the spectrum, they are neurodivergent, which means their brain works differently than a neurotypical brain.

Autism can impact their social, emotional and behavioral functioning. It's called a "spectrum disorder" because the range and severity of symptoms greatly vary.

Having a child with this diagnosis does not mean you did anything "wrong" during pregnancy or when your child was vaccinated to protect them against various diseases, or their nutrition/diet; or with the ways you treat, discipline and care for your child. Once you and your family accept this diagnosis with compassion, you can start moving forward to support your child's development and quality of life so they can function at their best in the world.

If you have a child diagnosed with autism, the great news is that we now know that the following strategies and accommodations can lead to children's greater functionality and adaptability.

1. Recognize functionality in the real world.

Consider how your child can function in the real world with the skills and abilities they have. If your child needs headphones to walk around the mall because of auditory overstimulation, that is a functional behavior. They are still going to the mall. When they are of age to pursue romantic relationships, they may choose to use dating apps to meet new people because it's less intimidating than meeting a potential partner in person. Always think of the ultimate goal (spend time at the mall; meet new people) and how your child's functional behaviors can make it possible in the real world.

2. Use a coach's mentality.

Coaches use an approach that teaches in a direct and goal-oriented manner. If you want your child to get better at a specific behavior or skill, teach them through modeling, practice and constructive feedback.

Use specific and non-sarcastic language. Great phrases to build in your repertoire include "When you say _____, it will make the other person feel _____."

3. Build a team.

When a team works together, things improve, whether we're talking about a Fortune 500 company or a basketball team. Your team is a support network that can consist of friends, family, coaches, tutors, therapists/counselors, teachers, babysitters, etc. Help your child with autism understand that working together as a team is better than working alone.

4. Practice makes better.

Take a "practice" approach instead of seeking perfection. This means that the goal of any change is to get better over time. By using this approach, the focus is not on your child's "failures" or challenges. Every action (positive or negative) is a practice toward improvement. Use growth mindset language, such as, "We're still working on it," or "You haven't learned that yet." Remind your child with autism about the skills they have already improved on over time and how far they've come toward doing the activities they want to do.

Learning that a loved one has been diagnosed with an autism spectrum disorder can be scary at first.

Most people in my generation still think of the movie *Rain Man* when they hear this diagnosis. However, society has moved toward understanding, accepting, and accommodating children and adults on the spectrum, and we still have a way to go. You and your family can make progress by creating the best environment at home for our loved ones with autism so they have the best chances for a successful and happy life beyond that environment.

Helpful Resources

Job Accommodation Network (JAN) is the leading source of free, expert and confidential guidance on job accommodations and disability employment issues. Serving customers across the United States and around the world for more than 35 years, JAN provides free one-on-one practical guidance and technical assistance on job accommodation solutions, Title I of the Americans with Disabilities Act (ADA) and related legislation, and self-employment and entrepreneurship options for people with disabilities.

Autism Speaks is dedicated to creating an inclusive world for all individuals with autism throughout their lifespan. The organization does this through advocacy, services, support, research and innovation, advancing care for autistic individuals and their families.

American Academy of Child & Adolescent Psychiatry provides information and online resources for children and teens with autism.

Helping Teenagers Build Healthy Relationships

Most of these articles are inspired by the children, teens and families I've worked with and have provided me with great insight into behavioral trends. One such area is the teenage relationship and how it's changed over the last thirty years. Teenage dating is not new. However, I've been fortunate enough to learn some new terms used during the courting stages like "mingling" or "talking" (FYI...mingling is physically being closer to the potential boyfriend/girlfriend without saying too much to each other while the talking stage is when they actually speak one-on-one with each other either over the phone or in person). What is new is social media, cell phones and fewer unsupervised areas. I've had the privilege of teens (boys and girls) feeling comfortable enough to share conversations they've had over text and a few consistent patterns have emerged. One observation is that teens who are about to date or are already in a relationship rely way too much on texting instead of talking. Two, there is an unhealthy amount of knowing what the other person is doing and where they are at all times. And finally, just like adult relationships, the most common problems arise from faulty communication and poor boundaries.

Having my own children, I'm fully aware that not all teens want to talk to their parents about their dating life. That's normal. That doesn't mean you avoid it at all costs. Instead, think of their first relationships as good practice for the last relationships they'll ever have (hopefully their future husband/wife/partner). Here are a few tips for helping your teens navigate their dating experiences:

1. Foster and model good communication.

Whenever possible, encourage your teens to TALK to their potential or current partner. It doesn't matter if it's in person or over the phone. Children and teens are missing or misinterpreting nuance (sarcasm, humor, anger, apathy, etc.) by not hearing others' voice tones and seeing nonverbal cues. Communication should also be open and honest and use productive communication with emphasis on communicating needs and goals (even communicating when they can't communicate calmly and effectively).

2. Normal discourse.

Teenagers love coming in and sharing that they are currently fighting with their partner.

When we analyze what that means, it typically means they got into some kind of argument that shouldn't have gone past a few minutes...maybe hours. Instead of looking at this as a normal occurrence in a relationship, they become very stressed thinking that any discourse is not expected. Remind them that part of any relationship, even just friendships, often has times of disagreement and that there is such a thing as healthy arguing (no name-calling, using sarcasm or manipulation, but instead healthy communication, sharing how they feel and what they need).

3. Boundaries. Define them, set them and stick with them.

While becoming upset over your partner's choice of dress, friends, leisure, etc., is also nothing new, tracking them online is. On more than one occasion, I've had a teen in a relationship tell me that they either check their partner's social media to see what they are wearing and if it is acceptable, or if they posted a pic with someone of the opposite sex and how they view it as a sign of disrespect. Have your teens talk to you about their own boundaries and expectations with you, including what they expect from each other, what are hard lines in the sand (being intimate with someone else) and what they need in order to continue to take care of themselves (self-care).

4. Balance.

During the beginning stages of a relationship, all those good hormones flood the brain, causing the new couple to only want to spend time with and talk to each other. While this happens, they might need to be encouraged to remember what else they need in their lives to be the best partner they can be. This can include time with friends, going to the gym, alone time, etc. They should also make sure their partner knows that balance doesn't mean being selfish. But rather, taking care of themself will only help the overall functioning of the relationship. This also ties into setting boundaries as teens often begin to focus more on their partner's needs than their own.

Teenage relationships are a great source of practice (and stress) for all future relationships.

There are just more complicating factors than previous generations. As parents and caregivers, we should use a mindset of growth when supporting these relationships. Even problems that arise from these relationships teach children and teenagers communication, boundaries and self-care. We should also be aware of our own children's developmental maturity and set our own limits regarding what kind of relationship they are ready for.

Medication and Children: Deciding If and When It Is Right for Your Child

Since the 1980s, there has been an increase in the diagnosis of childhood disorders that affect mood, attention, and hyperactivity. Most parents are curious if numbers are actually increasing, or if they are exacerbated by outside factors, such as increased school demands and screen time, inappropriate expectations and less time being physically active. The number of children with ADHD in the U.S. is roughly 10%, anxiety disorders 7% and depression 3%; however, this does not include children who are undiagnosed. These are pretty big numbers. Further research shows that children with untreated hyperactivity or mood disorders (anxiety and depression) live shorter lives because of increased unsafe and unhealthy behaviors (i.e., smoking, drinking, drug use, unhealthy diets, etc.), experience more difficulty obtaining and keeping a job, and have less successful relationships. So now what? Is medication the only option?

Here is some important information when considering medication for your child:

1. Know the data.

In recent reviews of anti-anxiety, antidepressant, and ADHD medication, it was found that ADHD medication is the most effective with the least amount of long-term side effects, but you should also update yourself on the latest research. This is not to say that it is a "magic pill," but the data is positive. For anti-anxiety and antidepressant medication, it was found that they are not as effective as once thought. In the 1970s and 1980s, studies were published showing these drugs should be the first line of defense when treating anxiety and depression; however, it was recently found that the drug companies did most of the studies, and only published studies that showed the drugs' effectiveness. Well-conducted research found that only Prozac was proven to be effective for children under the age of 18 with depression. So ask your doctors the right questions regarding what data they use when choosing one medication over another.

2. Look at all of the factors.

Many children are misdiagnosed for a myriad of reasons. One way to prevent this is to have a comprehensive evaluation including the child's history (birth, development, family, school, social, sleep, eating, exercise, etc.), current stressors, expectations and habits, observations of the child in different environments and information gathered from different people who have interactions with the child. The evaluation should include input from older children; however, most children with ADHD have difficulty rating their own behavior, which is why you want to gather as much information as possible. There are also strong genetic factors that doctors use when prescribing medication, meaning if a medication works for one or more close family members, there is a higher likelihood it will work for the child.

3. Step by step.

Deciding to have your child take medication can be very overwhelming and elicit feelings of guilt, anger and confusion. Try improving habits first, such as more consistent sleep schedules, plenty of exercise, a healthier diet, and less screen/game time in exchange for reading or playing games together. If symptoms don't improve over the next few weeks, you can then take the next step, which may be working with your child's school to accommodate or alleviate any potential causes for anxious or hyperactive symptoms.

4. Risk versus reward.

It is hard to be completely objective with your own child, which is why working with professionals will help you determine if the risk of medication is worth the reward of their overall improvement. If a child is suffering, meaning having thoughts of self-harm or suicide or feels that life is getting worse and worse, the risk is already high and greater than any possible side effects from a medication trial. If the child is only miserable at school, but happy everywhere else, the risk-reward analysis suggests you should begin by adjusting home and social-related factors.

Choosing whether or not to give your child medication for ADHD, anxiety or depression is an overwhelming and big decision for most parents. In order to make the best decision for your child, you must first know the facts. It is also very beneficial to have the right team you can collaborate with when making decisions regarding your child's mental health, medical and academic decisions. Unfortunately, there will be some trial and error as determining which medication is right for your child is not an exact science, so you will need to be patient. But while we may be an overmedicated nation, there are still plenty of children who eventually require at least a short-term regimen. And remember, while medication might be the right choice for your child, it doesn't always have to be the first choice.

Some more helpful information:

https://www.additudemag.com/choosing-adhd-professional-for-child-parenting/

https://childmind.org/article/what-parents-should-know-about-having-kids-on-multiple-medications/

Finding the Right Therapist for Your Child or Teen

It should be no surprise that the demand for mental health professionals is currently outpacing the supply. In economic models, this often leads to increased prices, but when it comes to healthcare, this can lead to taking what you can get. I've heard stories from children and parents about a poor fit between therapist and client and even inappropriate behavior and comments made by mental health professionals. Like any other profession, there will be variance among therapists. For children and teens, however, one of the most important factors is the relationship and rapport between client and therapist.

When choosing the right therapist for your child or teen, there are several important factors to consider. Below are some specific recommendations to increase your chances of a positive fit between your child or teen and their potential therapist:

1. You're the Customer.

If you take the view that you and your child are the customers and they are the salesman, you shift the hierarchy and dynamic in that you don't feel that you are lucky to get their business. Think of it like buying a house or car. You want to make sure they have the qualities you are looking for that fit best with your child or teen. A good first step is to ask close friends and family for their recommendations.

2. Goodness of Fit.

If you and your child know what types of personalities work best for them, this will make the process easier. Does your child work better with someone who is very practical and speaks openly or do they need someone who is more formal? Will they feel more comfortable with a man or woman? Also, feel free to ask how the therapist builds rapport with children and teenagers (i.e., play, interviews, shared interests, etc.).

3. Expertise and Experience.

Most importantly, does the therapist have the right areas of expertise and experience for what your child needs? Be sure to ask what they specialize in. If they tell you they specialize in "everything" or "working with children", ask for more specifics. Do they specialize in anxiety and/or depression? If so, what types of anxiety or depression and what therapeutic models do they use? Cognitive-behavioral, psychodynamic, solution-focused? Here is a link to definitions of different types of therapy:

https://www.aacap.org/AACAP/Families_and_Youth/Facts_for_Families/FFF-Guide/Psyc

hotherapies-For-Children-And-Adolescents-086.aspx

4. Sensitivities.

For many children, it will be important that they find a therapist who is sensitive to their identity, religion, culture, socioeconomic status, race, and family dynamics. If you have a child on the LGBTQ+ spectrum, make sure that there are no biases or beliefs that will cause any judgment or stress.

According to the most recent data, about half of all children and teens will require short- or long-term therapeutic intervention before they reach adulthood. While therapy itself is important, the fit between therapist and child/teen is equally, if not more so, important. If you remember this when finding the right therapist for your child, you'll increase the probability of a great collaboration.

Here are some helpful links if your child is in need of mental health treatment:

https://www.psychologytoday.com/us

https://psychcentral.com/lib/how-to-choose-the-right-therapist-for-your-child

Why Can't We Be Friends?

Helping Your Children Learn How to Initiate, Build and Maintain Friendships

"Nobody does that anymore... that is, like, so cringe!" One thing working with teenagers has taught me is new(ish) lingo. Another thing I've learned is that kids and teens are having more and more difficulty initiating conversations or friendships with one another.

In session, I often ask young people how they start talking to new peers. Does it happen organically while you're playing a sport or video game? Do you actually introduce yourself when meeting new classmates or teammates? Or do you just avoid the whole thing because it's "awkward" (their new favorite word)?

Many times, it's the latter. Young people are often too uncomfortable introducing themselves and striking up a conversation with other kids they don't know.

With the combination of helicopter parenting, over-scheduling and increased technology use, kids don't encounter enough opportunities to learn how to engage with one another. This leads to feelings of inadequacy that can become amplified as children get older.

Imagine your child has to enter a new high school where everyone has had their friend groups since elementary school. Or, your family moves to a new city before your child gains a lot of experience with social awareness and initiation.

Out of the three necessary skills that lead to strong relationships, initiating is the most difficult for kids and teens. They often don't know what to say or when to say it. More often than not, they rely on DM-ing or texting the new person, which provides a sense of anonymity, comfort and distance. They also share that they often wait until the other person initiates with them (no big secret, the other kid is doing the same avoidance technique).

Both teens in this situation are afraid of coming across as weird, desperate or dorky. But, the more times they avoid these face-to-face interactions, the more awkward they will feel about meeting new people and establishing new relationships.

How can you help your child overcome this form of social anxiety and start building new relationships with confidence? Share these tips with them.

1. Use your senses.

The first thing a person notices about another person is often what they're wearing, listening to, watching or playing. If you see someone with a shirt or piece of merch that is considered non-mainstream, the odds are they'll be excited to know you're into it, too. The same can be said for music or video games. Finding a common interest is a great start to a real connection.

2. Keep it going.

The easiest way to keep the conversation going without having to do all the talking yourself is to ask questions about whatever you used to initiate in the first place. If it was video games, find out what else they play, on what console and do they also like this other game that you're obsessed with right now. If music is your common ground, ask about concerts (who they've seen live or if they're going to any upcoming shows). Maybe they also play an instrument, produce music or sing. The idea is to show interest in what they're into, so you can share what you like, discover more common interests and hopefully find activities to do together sometime.

3. Disengage.

At some point, you're going to have to stop talking to each other. You don't have to ask for their Instagram account or phone number right away. In fact, you probably shouldn't, unless you feel an instant connection and want to keep this conversation going. What you can do is be friendly and vague by saying things like, "So, I gotta go, but I'll see you around" or, simply, "Later!"

4. Follow up.

Most kids and teens (and adults, for that matter) love when others show that they're thinking of them.

You can do this in a non-creepy way by either inviting them to something, sharing a funny meme or video with them or sending a simple message to remind them that you haven't forgotten about them.

By sharing these four tips with your child, you're making it clear that new friendships take some time, work and practice. Introducing themselves, finding common ground and following up can lead to more meaningful interactions when your child and their new acquaintance can make some shared memories and establish inside jokes that often lead to real friendships.

It's no secret that being a child or teenager in today's age has its difficulties – some of which you can't ease for them. While you can't be an intermediary and speak on behalf of your kid, you can give them some social tools to make the process more successful for them. Once they make it through a few new and maybe awkward social situations, friendships will grow and your child's confidence in new social situations will, too.

Stressed or Depressed?

How to Tell the Difference and What to do Next

With depression on the rise in American children, teens and young adults, it's important for parents to differentiate between a diagnosis of depression and/or anxiety disorder and the experience of acute (temporary) stress. While they often look and feel the same, there are a few specific differences. The similarities between stress and depression include changes in daily habits like sleep, eating and energy levels; feelings of anger and irritability; and difficulty with task initiation and concentration.

Depression is longer lasting and more serious than stress and often leads to characteristics such as not enjoying things one used to, trouble functioning in everyday life and even thoughts of suicide.

Stress, on the other hand, feels "bad," but it can be useful to motivate us to work harder to achieve goals. Long-term stress, however, and poor coping skills can eventually lead to depression.

Once you learn how to identify the warning signs in your child, you can help them learn and practice better coping skills so they can be well-equipped when these feelings arise in the future. Here are some helpful tips for identifying and coping with the early signs of stress and/or depression.

1. Start with the basics.

Most teens and young adults either don't get enough sleep and/or exercise or eat a healthy diet. These lifestyle habits can not only affect your child's mood and energy, they can even influence brain development; academic, social and athletic performance; and self-confidence. If your minor-aged children live in your home, set clear limits and boundaries. Turn off wi-fi at night and remove electronics from bedrooms to encourage quality sleep, require some physical activity each day (e.g., dog walking, cleaning, running errands, playing sports) and provide healthy snack and meal options at home.

2. Play detective.

When children and teens are dealing with a period of stress, it can be difficult for you and them to identify the triggers impacting their overall mental well-being. Consider what has changed in the last few weeks/months, and identify why they felt better in the past. For example, you may notice that since your child enrolled in a more difficult course load at school, they have less free time for friends and recreational activities. Or, maybe they've been thinking too much about negative national/global news they've seen on social media (e.g., wars, political discourse, school shootings). Understanding what triggered their depressive or anxious thoughts and feelings can help you and your child make positive changes.

3. Practice new coping skills.

Children are used to practicing for academic, physical (athletic), and creative (music, theater, visual arts) challenges and activities. So, it's a natural next step to have them learn and practice ways to self-regulate their emotions. There is no one-size-fits-all approach to this, so discover together what works best for them. Try daily mindful activities to help them stay "present" (in the moment) by focusing on what they're doing. Mindfulness practices include meditation (guided visualizations/meditations with an app, mindful journaling), creative sensory activities (coloring mandalas, sound scavenger hunt, freeze dancing, blindfold fruit tasting, active listening, tea ceremony), and physical exercises (meditative walking, yoga, breathing exercises like box breathing, blowing bubbles). They can also benefit from learning how to ask for help (e.g., "I'm feeling _____ and I need _____.").

4. It takes a village.

We're not often taught to ask for help and are left thinking that we have to do everything on our own.

Shift your thinking as a parent to consider the benefits of having support. Create a team that you can turn to (and who can turn to you), including friends and family, professionals from your child's school or within the community, and even online support groups. Regardless of what your child is going through, someone on your team can relate or share an experience or advice that helps you see a challenge from a different perspective or learn how to approach it in a new way.

Stress is a natural part of life. But, if unchecked and left to fester, it can lead to longer-lasting problems.

By teaching your child how to cope better with the child's day-to-day stressors, you can increase the likelihood that their stress doesn't eventually lead to a depression diagnosis.

Helpful Resources

Apps

Dare

Youper

Videos

Institute for Positive Education

New Horizon - Meditation and Sleep Stories

Teens, Screens and Depression

Teen depression is up. Teen isolation is up. Teen screen usage is also up. Study after study has tried to understand the relationship between social media usage and the increased rates of depression in teenagers, and several conclusions are apparent.

• Rates of depression have been steadily increasing since the invention of the smartphone.

• Schools and homework require more screen time, making it harder for teens to engage in non-technologically dependent activities.

• Teens are less independent and aren't free to roam the city or their neighborhoods like previous generations.

There is no definitive study saying increased screen usage "causes" depression. However, there is an important nuance regarding children. Many children who already have rich social lives and healthy self-esteem often use social media to enhance their social lives. On the other hand, children who already exhibit signs of depression, have limited social interactions and experience feelings of inadequacy may rely on the internet for all of their social needs. This often deepens feelings of depression, increases lack of engagement and further lowers already poor motivation.

One thing we know for sure about adolescence is that teenagers need to be with their peers in person, engaging in unstructured activities like going to the mall, hanging out at a friend's house and road trips.

Parents have never had more to worry about regarding their child's safety. However, keeping teens at home or only doing structured activities like sports is not a solution. Limiting their time outside and with friends deprives kids of meaningful opportunities to be themselves in various environments, deepen connections with their peers, and make mistakes.

How can you reconsider your child's screen usage and social life to support their mental well-being?

1. Set some limits.

Tik-Tok, Instagram or Snapchat will never alert your child if they've been online for too long, even when they really could benefit from putting down their phone, tablet or laptop. Setting these limits is your job.

Think of this like speed limits and credit card spending limits for adults. You can set very specific limits to screen usage and explain to your child (when they give you an attitude) that science says they need limits. A good rule of thumb is the 1:1 ratio (1 hour of screen time requires 1 hour of screen-free time that's not a nap or bedtime). You can also establish screen-free activities like family meal times, when they have friends over, on family vacations, or during family discussions.

2. Replace screentime with activity.

If your child is more engaged in meaningful activities, they will be less inclined to grab their phone.

Having a part-time job, creative or athletic hobbies, more household duties or friends over at the house can be rewarding and productive. To make this an easier choice for your teen, be available to drive your child(ren) to these activities at least once a week.

3. Encourage your child to find their purpose.

As children become adults, many have a difficult time staying motivated and engaged and often turn to social media as an escape. Having a sense of purpose will not only increase their motivation, it will also improve their overall self-worth. Seeking their sense of purpose can be as simple as volunteering or trying a new hobby or as complex as starting their own business. It starts with encouraging your child to explore their interests and not be afraid to fail.

4. Lead by example.

We've all fallen into the trap of telling our kids to "do what we say and not what we do." Unfortunately, children see their parents' behaviors as silent approval of them. Without realizing it, teens can excuse their own unhealthy habits when they're simply doing what they see at home. When setting your child's limits for screen time, establish your own limits, as well. Explain to your adolescent kid that even adults have difficulty ignoring or turning off their devices. By having healthy and honest communication (not yelling and nagging) about this topic, you will be more in tune with their warning signs of overuse. And your kids won't forget to remind you to put down your phone at dinner, too.

Social media isn't going away. In fact, it will probably keep evolving and intertwining into our everyday functioning. That's why it's essential to teach our children how to establish a healthy screen-life balance with realistic boundaries, much like the work-life balance we all strive for.

Get a Job: The Long-Term Benefits of Work

For previous generations, having a job while going to school was common. Whether working at the mall, a grocery store, for a family friend, or babysitting, teenagers experienced many benefits from balancing school, work and friends. Most parents I encounter state that they would rather their children concentrate on school and/or after-school activities. What is forgotten are the invaluable experiences teens experience at a job. Forget about the money and staying out of trouble (which are added bonuses), they also have to practice time management, learn about a corporate structure, build relationships with peers and supervisors, learn more about their own interests and dislikes and for some, lead to future careers. One of the biggest rewards of having a job is learning how to be more responsible. Here are some ideas on having children and teens learn about the benefits of having a job while in school:

1. Start 'em young.

Kids as young as 2 can have jobs around the house. You can start with small jobs such as putting their bath toys away, dirty clothes in the hamper, or dirty silverware in the sink. You do or don't have to tie this in with allowance; however, an allowance does help children learn about budgeting, delaying gratification (if you make them use their own money to buy things they want, not need), and financial responsibility (not wasting money on things they stop using after one day).

2. Quality over quantity.

Teens are lucky enough to be born into a time in which there is flexibility in the workforce. Many jobs allow employees to work one day a week or only on the weekends. Even if your child works 5 hours/week, they would be getting something out of it... including putting something on a resume when they get older.

3. Good for their health.

Mental health literature often talks about mentally healthy individuals feeling connected with others and feeling a part of a community. Teenagers often find themselves isolating more when they are stressed or overwhelmed mostly secluding themselves in their rooms with social media and Netflix. Having a job creates the acceptance and camaraderie that promotes mental health.

4. Think outside the box.

A job doesn't have to look like it did in the 1950s with a paper route or working as a soda jerk. There are enough opportunities that if a child wants to work from their computer, in an office, outdoors, or in a traditional store, there are availabilities for them. Use websites such as indeed.com, hireteen.com, or snag.com.

Many CEOs, presidents of companies and those hiring new employees all agree that the new generation of young adults are lacking in skills that can often be obtained by having a job. From interviewing (what to wear, eye contact, listening, body language) to on-the-job problem solving, children can learn just as much from an after-school job as from an AP European History class (no offense to AP Euro). If you're concerned about them juggling a job with school demands, maybe there needs to be more balance in their lives, so that they become more mentally healthy, and experienced young adults.

Doing What You Love or Loving Who You're With: How Important is it to Love Your Job?

Over the last century, more and more high school graduates have now been deciding to go to college after high school. They are all faced with the decisions of what major and, eventually career to pursue. For many, this has become a great source of stress and apprehension. It's folly to think most 18-year-olds will have any idea of what they want to do for the next forty years. They are given messages from family, social media and influencers to "do what they love" or to "find their passion." I don't know about you, but I haven't met many people who are passionate about computer science or accounting. They might enjoy the work, sure, but passionate? Teens have been presented with this unrealistic goal of finding what they love to do and turning it into a profitable career.

That is a lot of pressure. So much pressure that many become overwhelmed and paralyzed when thinking about selecting their major(s) in college. As parents and trusted adults, we can alleviate some of that pressure. Instead of focusing so much on doing what they love (many don't even know yet), focus on finding a culture or environment that fosters comradery and connectivity. Here are some easy ways to help high school and college-aged students shift their thinking and alleviate some of the unnecessary anxiety when choosing a career:

1. Time.

Remind your children that finding what they enjoy takes time and if they don't, that's ok!

Most college students change their major, need an extra semester or two, or eventually work outside of their field of study. What's the rush? Equating time to a commodity, they're better suited to spending a few extra semesters on the front end figuring it out than discovering they hate their career choice and having to start from scratch.

2. Love The One You're With.

Most job satisfaction surveys reveal that people value who they work with more than the work itself. Does your child prefer a smaller, close-knit environment or a larger setting with hundreds of employees? Do they like a more informal setting or one with specific rules and routines? Have they considered jobs or careers that provide them with in-person collaboration rather than remote work?

3. Start Building Relationships.

With the rise of social media, over-scheduling, parents' anxiety about kids being out and about and dependence on technology, many children aren't given opportunities to build meaningful and lasting relationships. Instead of primarily focusing on grades or after-school activities, prioritize building and maintaining lasting, meaningful relationships.

4. What If?

Let's say your child eventually ends up in a job or career they don't love, or they don't love the people with whom they are working. Guess what? They can always look for something else or at least talk to their supervisors about changing what they do or who they connect with on a daily basis. This further gives them opportunities to self-advocate and problem-solve, which will serve them well in all other areas of life.

For years, students have been focusing so much on getting good grades or making it through high school that they've neglected to think of the bigger picture regarding their life and career.

While some young adults want to find a career or job they are passionate about, others just want to make enough money to pay the rent and have some fun. It is not possible for every future professional to feel passionate about their job or career. That's ok. So if they don't fall in love with what they do, hopefully they can love the people with whom they work.

ACADEMIC PERFORMANCE

How Does My Child Learn Best?

During COVID, parents had more direct observations of their children's learning prowess in real-time and were either more encouraged or more worried about their aptitude. It is important to point out that children have never before been asked to learn in a virtual format. Brains have been wired to learn via in-person human-to-human interaction or experiential learning. That is learning by doing. Thrown in the discrepancy between the evolution of brain development and technological advancement and what we learned is that most children still learn best by learning from and with other humans.

In school psychology, we are trained to understand and assess how children think, learn, reason and problem-solve. By learning how children learn best, we can better equip stakeholders in their education as well as children themselves to use what works best. How can we expect parents to work, take care of the house and ensure their children are learning in an environment with more and more distractions? This is not a knock on the school system. Before COVID, there was no preparation to deal with the digital divide, working parents and the stress of a national pandemic all at once.

If we tweak our mindset a little and use COVID as an experiential process, we actually learn a lot. Some of us are learning that our children work better from home with fewer distractions and with the ability to work at their own pace. Some have learned that our children need more structure to accomplish tasks (i.e., schedules, set break times, checklists, etc.). What most of us have learned is that each child has their own strengths and weaknesses and that we can use that knowledge to improve our child's chances for success.

Here are a few quick tips to help your child discover what works best for them:

1. Use the data.

It's hard enough for teachers who are trained in child learning and development to determine how children learn best, so as parents, we need to use any data we can get our hands on. There are formal data, which are test scores (standardized like state testing or scores from classroom tests) and informal data, which can be observations, notes from the teacher, patterns in how children learn new information and so on. What's also helpful regarding data is that it is more objective than children's or parents' opinions.

2. Visual, auditory, hands-on or all three.

For years, there has been the belief that people learn best by one modality (visualizing, listening or doing). It is usually more complicated than that. For many children, it depends on the task. Others may have to use one sensory input at a time (Listen to the lecture first, then go back and read the notes). Work with your child as a team to determine which modality works best for specific subjects and assignments.

Does your child need to use videos to study history but do practice problems to study math? Should they study with peers because they need to talk it out or do they need to use game-based instruction because it is easier to sustain attention and motivation?

3. One big experiment.

Instead of forcing them to do things your way, have them try different ways to learn and work and use the data to help them discover if their strategies are working. In framing work this way, you may get more buy-in and not be told how "annoying" you are for constantly telling them to study. Look back at previous grades and analyze what worked and what didn't. For most, it will be a combination of their interest, motivation, learning strengths and weaknesses and teachers.

4. Get more information.

If your child is still having difficulty after implementing different interventions and strategies, it is probably time to get additional information by having a comprehensive evaluation. Most clinical and school psychologists are trained to assess a child's learning aptitude, including measures of cognition, executive functioning, memory, attention and academic skills. While public schools can provide this service, it is incumbent upon the parents to advocate for an evaluation if their child is not making adequate progress. You can also find a private psychologist by doing a search on Psychology Today or through your insurance company's website.

Any parent can tell you that no two children are alike. This goes for their learning styles as well as their personalities. Schools have honed their skills in teaching the 3 Rs (reading, 'riting, 'rithmetic) but are still lacking when it comes to teaching children how they learn best. Parents and other professionals are going to have to fill the gap in the meantime, so by focusing on "how" children learn instead of "what" they learn, we can ensure they are better equipped to solve any problems that come their way in school... but more importantly, in life.

Getting Reluctant Readers to Read More

Research has consistently shown for decades that one of the greatest predictors of academic success is the amount a child reads. The more a child or teenager reads, the better they perform in math, history, science and language arts. Unfortunately, not every child likes to read or may even have deficits such as learning or attention disorders that make reading feel more like a punishment than a source of creativity and imagination.

There are also those who can read just fine, just choose not to for a number of reasons... mostly it's not as entertaining as a phone, computer or television.

Most elementary schools around the country assign a specific number of minutes to be read by children, but this often stops once they reach middle school. I frequently find out from students in middle and high school that they are not assigned novels to read on their own and/or during class, focusing more on reading short passages with the purpose of getting ready for state-mandated tests. Even though there are more distractions and reasons for children not to read, there are more options than ever in the course of history to find high-interest literature for all ages and reading levels. If you have a child who is reluctant to read, here are a few ways to get them to develop the habit:

1. Whatever they like.

That's right! It's more important that your child reads, even if you don't find it

Interesting or meaningful. Find out what their main interests are and there is no doubt you will find a book or many books about it. Use the 5-finger rule when determining if the book is on their reading level (they should get no more than 5 words incorrect on a page when reading it aloud or to themself). This goes for magazines, newspapers, etc.

2. Model.

Parents should find time every day to dedicate at least 10-20 minutes of quiet reading time. This can be done as a family, with your partner or on your own. Discuss the book with your child (if appropriate) and have them tell you what they're reading about.

3. Start small.

If your child doesn't read at all, don't expect them to start by reading twenty minutes each night. Have them start with a page or two. If you prefer time, have them read for a set amount of minutes. You'll want to make sure they're actually reading so it would help to know the reading material yourself first.

4. Listening can be just as useful as reading.

Many parents have asked over the years if audiobooks are ok and not to oversimplify the answer, but yes, listening to a book is better than nothing. It's even better if your child follows along in the book while listening to the audio format. Over time, you can begin alternating where they might listen to a few pages and then read a few on their own.

With all of the advances in technology and research on teaching and learning, there is still no substitute for reading. It's also easier than ever to access free reading materials online or in person around the country. We quickly forgot that one asset our local taxes pay for is public libraries—libraries that often have staff who can help get you and your family on the right track to make reading a daily habit.

What the EF? The Importance of Executive Functioning in Your Child's Success

Education and psychology often have "buzzwords" that obtain popularity through social media, news outlets, books and research. Terms such as self-esteem, positive reinforcement and entitlement have been uttered by millions of parents and educators over the years, but has talking about these topics helped our children? In short, it depends. If it has changed how we teach and parent for better outcomes for our children, then yes. A new buzzword that is more important now than ever is "executive functioning."

Think of the executive functions like the manager in your brain. This regulator process is making sure all parts are working together to achieve a common goal. Executive functions or EF include managing time, organizing yourself and tasks, paying attention, prioritizing, being flexible and inhibiting your responses. It also includes how you plan your behaviors and regulate your emotions. When thinking of our children, many of these skills don't fully develop until our late teens or early twenties, but it doesn't mean we can't learn and improve these skills while they are still developing.

With increased emphasis on test scores and GPAs, we shouldn't forget that without EF skills, our children wouldn't last more than a week on their own. Research from Fortune 500 companies reveals that they would prefer employees with great social and EF skills to employees primarily with strong GPAs obtained from Ivy League schools. So here are some tips to help improve your children's EF skills:

1. Practice, practice, practice.

Like any other skill you want to improve, there is no better way than to practice. It is important that children not only practice these skills, but practice them correctly with support and feedback. Some examples include:

a. If they are working on increasing how much homework they can do on their own without getting distracted, have them start by either doing 3-5 minutes alone or the first 5 items before you check in with them. You can increase the amount of time or work to be completed while decreasing your involvement over time

b. Have them plan more things on their own like dinner, get-togethers with friends, aspects of a vacation, etc.

c. Encourage your children to generate their own solutions to problems by asking them what their plan is if something doesn't work out

2. Talk it out.

By modeling what these skills look and sound like, they will start to internalize the necessary language and skills to apply their own EF strategies. Talk about how long things might take, use your own calendars and checklists or tell them how you plan on prioritizing things such as getting dinner ready, leaving the house on time, etc.

3. Meaningful consequences.

Children who have difficulty with executive functioning skills often require external support such as rewards or praise and don't learn as well from their mistakes. That is why these kids are often labeled as "lazy" or "unmotivated." They will need your continued support as they continue to strengthen these skills. Examples may include play breaks after work periods, changing locations to complete work and immediate reinforcement for the desired behavior.

4. Thinking about thinking.

Metacognitive approaches can be very helpful when teaching children how to learn what works and what doesn't. This will also help with buy-in when getting your children to practice EF skills. Use terms such as "this seems to work better" or "what is a different way we can do this" when implementing EF strategies.

For decades, parents and educators have focused on teaching reading, writing and math. Now it is time for us to start working on the behaviors that allow children to apply what they've learned by becoming independent adults. Unlike many buzzwords over the years, this one (EF) will actually lead to lifelong benefits and unless you're ready to move into your child's dorm rooms or apartments, it's time we start teaching these skills early and often.

Identifying and Preventing School Burnout

As the school year trudges on, students of all ages begin to experience some kind of fatigue that is evident based on their behaviors and reactions. For high school seniors, the end of the school year is the final chapter in their educational lives as they know it. Soon they will be given more freedom than they've ever had. For younger children, the final few months leading up to summer often include end-of-year testing, field trips and/or the pressure of bringing up lower grades. All of these age groups have one thing in common, they can begin feeling burnt out.

Burnout can be identified as a negative emotional, physical, or behavioral change caused by prolonged school-related activities that are often stressful. These can include homework, studying, projects, quizzes and tests as well as the daily grind of day-to-day school expectations. Burnout often causes symptoms such as low motivation, difficulty getting started on tasks, distractibility and irritability. It can also lead to having less energy and a lower tolerance for run-of-the-mill problems.

The good news is after identifying it, there are specific actions we can take to help our children if they are experiencing school burnout:

1. Look for the clues.

If it looks like a duck and quacks like a duck...you know the rest. When a child or teenager is missing assignments or forgetting to turn in work and is avoiding any school-related activities and this is not typical for them, that's a red flag. Other red flags can be increased isolation, irritability and lying about school work. Another effective way to determine if your child is feeling burnt out is to rule out other possible causes for these behaviors (i.e., social dilemma, serious mental health struggle, environmental stressors like divorce, or major changes in family structure).

2. Communicate (without nagging).

We are all guilty of micromanaging, or from a child's perspective, nagging. Use nonjudgmental language when talking with your child. Examples can include saying things like, "This doesn't seem to be working" or "It looks like it's really hard for you to get started, do you want to try something else?" Also, encourage them to communicate with others, including their teachers, counselors or friends to help brainstorm ideas to deal with any stressors that are getting in the way of their optimal performance.

3. Balance.

Burnout is often a red flag that there is too much mental energy or emphasis placed on school and should be looked at as a warning sign, not a stop sign. Help your child figure out ways to introduce more balance in their lives by making better use of their "work" time (see article on screens and teens) and fun time. There should be dedicated social time and downtime each day along with a healthy amount of non-academic activities like part-time jobs, sports, hobbies, etc.

4. Brainstorm.

A friend once told me that, "We are bigger than any problem." Wow! Talk about empowering. Any problem, in this instance burnout, can be looked at as just another problem we get to solve. Solutions should include your team (parents, teachers, therapists, coaches, etc.) and focus on realistic solutions. Maybe your child's level of classes is too difficult, or the homework load is too great. Include your child in this process so they feel like they are in the game and not on the bench.

Like life, school is a marathon, not a race and requires frequent analysis and flexibility to be successful. Parents and children can learn how to manage and even prevent symptoms of school burnout by identifying, communicating and problem-solving together.

Improving School Performance in Disengaged and Unmotivated Students

An 8th-grade client recently came back for therapy after going to military school during the pandemic. He was recently suspended for using some colorful language with peers and is failing all of his classes as he's been to at least three different schools in the last three years and is receiving accommodations for ADHD. Something is not working. We've focused on his goals, motivation and causes for school avoidance and poor academic performance and discovered the following: he doesn't see how anything he is learning will be useful for the future, doesn't find any of the information interesting, feels that teachers only use punishment as a consequence and is overwhelmed by how much work is assigned. He's only fifteen and ready to drop out of school.

This teenage boy is lucky enough to have a mother who is a strong advocate to help him get what he needs, but at what point do we have to think of the bigger picture? Maybe traditional school is not for him. Maybe we have to focus on his outside activities to help him become more engaged in school and hopeful for his future. While options for children like this are not perfect, there are still many ways to "find what works" when thinking about their education and future. Unfortunately, this boy is not alone. There are tens of thousands of students each year who become more disengaged and unmotivated with their parents and teachers resorting to punishment and negative consequences (which usually do not work). Here are some ideas for collaborating with these children to increase their likelihood of success in the future:

1. Think outside the box.

Traditional school is not for everyone. Not every child has to go to college or even a typical high school. There are many options including technical high schools, home schools and hybrid models that offer certifications in areas from computer science to culinary arts and home improvement. Some children might perform better if they enroll in virtual school while having a part time job that prepares them for their future.

2. Non-school related activities.

Sometimes, less is more. Focus on life outside of school by having your child either get a part-time job (if old enough), having more opportunities to see classmates outside of school or finding something that is of great interest to them. Children and teens are great researchers of information and will often successfully find opportunities when given several choices (i.e. working at a restaurant or bookstore, volunteering at an animal shelter or a park, etc.).

3. Connecting with a team.

If your child has no other choice but to stay in their current academic setting, begin collaborating and building relationships with all stakeholders in your child's future. This can include school counselors, teachers, coaches, administrators, etc. Make sure your child feels that they are part of the team by including them whenever possible and encouraging honest and open dialogue.

This will help with problem-solving and your child feeling more invested in their learning and future.

4. Finding what works.

Instead of worrying about the here and now, focus communication in terms of what is or is not working for their future. Remind your child (and yourself) that this is a process and may take some time; however, the goal is finding what works best to increase future success. This will also reduce the amount of negative interactions and communication your child is exposed to.

Eventually your child will be able to say to you, their teacher and one day, their boss, "This isn't working and I think we need to try something different."

School success isn't only related to a child's intelligence or how much money their parents make. School success also cannot be measured by good grades and standardized test scores.

For those children who aren't built to sit in a classroom for six to seven hours a day listening to adults lecture them on concepts that mean nothing to them, we must think outside the box and find alternative ways when preparing them for the future.

Hitting the Gas or Pumping the Brakes: Helping Children Succeed Without Burning Out

According to what is known as "The Yerkes-Dodson law," performance increases with physiological or mental arousal (stress) but only up to a point. When the level of stress becomes too high, performance decreases. This is especially true for children and teens. Our society has been putting more and more pressure (or stress) on children starting at younger ages. Thirty years ago, kindergarten was meant to learn the alphabet, how to raise your hand and make friends. Now, parents are worried if their children aren't reading before leaving pre-k. High-stakes testing, over-scheduling and increased academic rigor continue to place unnecessary stress on children and teens. And it is showing. Most studies show that about half of all children and teens say they have experienced significant anxiety or depression that year.

Let's be clear. This is not normal...especially in children. Children should be worried about hitting a fastball or if they're ready for their talent show, not if they can pass an end-of-the-year test. A healthy amount of stress or arousal is necessary for performance and success, but too much or too little does not work. That is where we come in! We (the adults) should help our children find the right amount of pressure in each area of their lives to be as successful as they can be without suffering the consequences of too much (or too little) stress. Here are a few ideas for helping children learn when they need to increase their effort or scale it back:

1. Promote and Model Balance.

Fostering a work-play balance from a young age helps children develop their own boundaries for self-care. Examples can range from social and alone time to technology and non-tech time. Parents can set these routines early by modeling it for them. Examples include no technology while eating as a family, daily walks, reading before bed, etc.

2. Life is a marathon, not a sprint.

It helps to let children know (especially overachieving students) that if they keep the metaphorical gas pedal down for too long and if they push too hard, they'll burn out. It is also beneficial to teach them that by finding a healthy balance, they'll be more efficient and eventually more satisfied with their lives. Help them also learn their own warning signs of being overwhelmed, such as changes in behavior, attitude and satisfaction with hobbies.

3. Reframe those negative thoughts

If I had a nickel each time a high school student told me that by failing a test, they ruined their future, I'd have accumulated quite a bit of money actually. Use real-life examples of your own failures and that they often didn't have the long-term consequences they think they do. A fun activity is to ask if their performance or test grade will matter in five days, weeks, months and years.

4. An ounce of prevention.

By promoting self-care from an early age, we can prevent most burnout and mental health problems. However, even self-care should have balance and limits. Watching online videos may be fine, but watching for seven straight hours when you have a lot of homework is just avoidance, not self-care. A great technique is to combine self-care and productivity. Listening to your favorite music while doing schoolwork, studying with friends, or doing homework in a fun environment can alleviate pressure and increase work output.

By all measures, this generation is one of the most stressed and anxious we've had since we began measuring mental well-being. Therefore there should be an emphasis on helping children and teens learn how to find their optimal level of stress and arousal to perform at their best without eventually burning out. Because mental health issues are often caused by multiple factors that are difficult to control, let's focus on helping our children learn how to recognize and manage their own stress… who knows, maybe we'll learn a few things from them as well.

College? You Still Need Me to Wake You Up! Fostering Independence in Your Soon-To-Be Adults

I have worked with college professors lamenting about parents emailing them to excuse their child's missed assignment or give them another chance to take a test in which they missed or failed. When determining if your child is ready for college, it's not only about getting good grades. For some, that's the easiest part. The harder part is having the independent skills that will keep your child in college and eventually living as a real-life ADULT. My sister once introduced me to the term "adulting," which I define as "making decisions, solving problems and navigating the daily situations that arise requiring focus, attention, and objectivity." In other words, we can't depend on our parents or other adults to solve our problems for us. We can, however, work collaboratively with others to get our needs met and goals achieved.

With the increased focus on test scores, extracurricular activities and grades, not enough energy and time has gone into teaching basic life skills to survive after high school. For the past 50 years, the number of high school students who also have a part-time job has steadily decreased. Observationally, so has the number of teenagers who know how to drive, prioritize their workload and leave the comfort of their bedrooms. Before your children go off on their own, it's imperative they learn how to survive on their own.

Here are some helpful strategies to help build independent living skills in your children and teens:

1. Start with the basics.

Can your child wake up on their own? Do they know when to go to sleep so they will feel rested and alert the following day? Do they make sure they have a balanced diet? Do they get some exercise and not just stay indoors all day? Can they recognize when someone is trying to take advantage of them? Start with health and safety. If they have good healthy habits, they are on the right track. If not, it's never too late to start.

2. If you left them alone for a week.

If you left your teen alone for a week, would they be able to survive? This is a great question as a baseline determinant when assessing your child's independence skills. Can they be safe and know what to do if something goes wrong (i.e., air conditioning or car breaking down)? Would they get themselves to school and complete their work?

3. Let them solve their own problems.

In the example above, the professor is agitated because the parents are contacting them, not the students themselves. Let your child start early with problem-solving activities, including effective communication, trying out different solutions, weighing risks versus rewards, learning when to ask for help and knowing how to find people who know more than them.

4. College isn't for everyone, but everyone should be educated.

Hopefully this information isn't segregating the population of families whose children will not attend a traditional 4-year university. Many teens will go to trade school, enroll in the military, police or fire academy or enter the workforce. The same skills apply to these young adults for their future success. The only difference is that some post high school environments have the structure in place so you can't sleep in late (morning revelry) or skip class.

Success in adult life is not directly related to the level of intelligence or how many AP classes your child takes in high school. Some better predictors of future success are executive skills, such as planning, time management, initiating tasks, etc., social skills and problem-solving abilities. Many of these skills have to be taught and practiced, and won't happen overnight. By the time our children reach high school, our focus should be more on how they function independently instead of their GPA, SAT scores, or AP credits.